AN

ESSAY

ON

TEMPTATION.

BY

E. C. WINES, D.D.

PHILADELPHIA:
PRESBYTERIAN BOARD OF PUBLICATION,
No. 821 Chestnut Street.

STEREOTYPED BY WESTCOTT & THOMSON.

CONTENTS.

CHAPTER IV.

CHAPTER V.

CHAPTER VI.

PAGE

CHAPTER VII.

CHAPTER VIII.

CHAPTER IX.

CHAPTER X.

AN ESSAY ON TEMPTATION.

CHAPTER I.

PLAN OF THE WORK.

TEMPTATION! What is it? From what sources does it spring? Wherein lies its strength? Is it to be looked for by all? Can it be resisted? What is it to endure temptation? By what helps is it to be endured? What grounds of encouragement are open to the tempted? Is deliverance sure to the tempted believer? What general lessons are conveyed by the Scripture doctrine of temptation? What special lessons are to be drawn from the more signal examples of temptation recorded in Holy Scripture?

These interrogatories indicate, in a general way, the line of thought to be pursued in the following pages. They present an outline of the chief points, which it is proposed to embrace in our inquiries and meditations on the general subject of temptation.

May the Divine Spirit graciously afford all needed aid to both the writer and the reader;—to the former, that he may indite, upon the important topics to be treated, only what is true and fitting; to the latter, that he may receive and profit by the truth so exhibited.

CHAPTER II.

THE NATURE OF TEMPTATION.

In the brief but comprehensive directory for prayer, left us by our blessed Lord, this petition occurs: "Lead us not into temptation." A marked peculiarity of the Christian religion is found in the prayers recorded in its sacred books. These prayers, unlike those of every system of false religion, are founded on a true philosophy of man. They enter into the very depths of our moral nature. They spring from our necessities. They are adapted to our mental constitution. They recognize our character and circumstances as transgressors. They enter into our feelings and our fears. They teach us our wants and our dangers.

Of the truth of this view, we have a signal proof in the petition just cited: "Lead us not into temptation." This is, peculiarly and pre-eminently, a Christian petition. It relates to a subject, on which every other religion is silent; a subject, whose truth and importance every Christian knows, and many deeply feel who are ignorant of the consolations of Christian hope.

The Essential Idea, inhering in the word Temptation, is Trial; putting a thing to the Test.

This is the primary meaning of the term in the original language of the New Testament. The word is applied both to material objects and rational beings; and that with the same general meaning.

It is applied to material objects. Thus metals are tried by subjecting them to the fire, to discover what degree of purity or alloy belongs to them. A cannon is tried by discharging balls from it, to see whether it is sound and may be safely used, or whether some flaw exists in it, which will render it useless. The strength of a rope is tried by attaching different weights to it, to ascertain how much it will bear, or what momentum it will resist.

But the word is also applied to rational beings. Thus a man's intellect is tried, by applying it to different questions. A man's will is tried, by subjecting it to various motives. A man's moral qualities are tried, by putting him in a variety of situations, where those qualities will be subjected to different agencies.

Temptation, then, is that which tries a man's strength. It is that which discovers his temper. It is that which reveals his power of will. It is that which shows, both to himself and others, the moral bias of his soul. In a word, it is that which draws out and makes manifest what is within him. Both prosperous circumstances in providence and adverse circumstances alike do this. Hence the apostle James says: "My brethren, count it all joy, when ye fall into *divers* temptations."

There is scarcely anything which we meet with in the world, scarcely any event which befalls us in providence, in which there is not some tempting power; something which tries our strength, discovers our disposition, and reveals what is in us. But there is, especially, a great tempting faculty in things which are more eminent in their nature. For example: High public trusts try men's integrity. Prosperity tries their humility. Afflictions try their faith. Injuries try their meekness. Vexations try their patience. These things, as an old writer has quaintly but aptly expressed it, "stir the water that was possibly clear at the top, and so try whether it be not muddy at the bottom."

Such, then, is the general idea embodied in the word temptation.

But the Term is often used in a more Restricted Sense, viz. to denote Occasions and Provocations to Sin.

It is, perhaps more frequently than otherwise, applied to designate some influence, which, directly and by its own nature, draws men to a transgression of the divine law. This influence may be of circumstances: in this case, men are said to be tempted by the world. It may be of an intelligent agent, directly enticing them to evil: in this case, they are tempted by the devil. Or it may be of their own carnal nature: and in this case, they are under temptation by the flesh.

Our Saviour, we have seen, teaches us to offer this prayer to God: "Lead us not into temptation." The petition is not to be interpreted as implying that God, by a positive influence, ever does, or can, directly incline men to evil; a notion as irrational as it is wicked. It does, however, undoubtedly pre-suppose that, under the governance of his providence, we may be exposed to temptation from the sources just noticed, and that we may be more exposed to it at some times than we are at others. It seems still further to imply that God may, in his own sovereign wisdom, and for his own glorious and holy ends, suffer us to be brought, at times, into circumstances of peculiar trial and danger.

Against temptation of every kind and in every degree, as an evil to be deprecated, our Lord teaches us to pray. But in this, as in other instances of such general and absolute requests, there is always a silent reserve for the divine will and wisdom, when they shall determine otherwise. In such a case, the spirit of the petition, as our catechism instructs us, implores a gracious support under the temptation, and a final deliverance out of it.*

* Dr. South's explication of the word temptation, which agrees substantially with that given in the text, is as follows: "The other thing to be inquired into and explained by us is, what is here

meant by 'temptation;' a thing better known by its ill effects, than by the best description. The Greek word is *peirasmos*, which signifies *trial*, and so imports not so much the matter as the end of the dispensation. So that anything whatsoever, which tends to try and discover what is in the heart or will of man, is and may be (in one respect or other) called a 'temptation.' In which sense outward crosses and afflictions are so called, and the people of God are bidden by the apostle 'to rejoice when they fall into divers temptations.' Jas. i. 2. And, according to the several ways and methods whereby God draws forth and discovers what is lodged in the hearts of men, good or bad, God himself is said to 'tempt them;' that is, to *try* or *prove* them. In which respect he was said to have *tempted* Abraham, in Gen. xxii. 1. But (the common and most received use of the word having added something of malignity to its first and native signification) generally in Scripture it denotes not only a bare trial, but such a one as is attended with a design to hurt or mischieve the people so tried. In which sense the Scribes and Pharisees are so often brought in by the Evangelists as tempting our Saviour; that is, they were still trying him with captious, ensnaring questions, as we find in Luke xi. 54, and elsewhere, 'to get something out of his mouth to accuse and destroy him.' But, chiefly and most frequently, the Scripture means by it such a trial as is intended to supplant and ruin a man in his spiritual concerns by inducing him to sin, and so subjecting him to the fatal effects and consequences thereof. And thus, on the contrary, it is said of God that he 'tempts no man,' in Jas. i. 13. This sort of temptation always proceeding from a man's own inherent corruption and concupiscence, set on work by their trusty confederate and co-worker the devil, whose peculiar province and perpetual business being to tempt men this way, he has, accordingly, by way of eminence, appropriated the odious name of 'tempter' to himself. And, therefore, to give a full account of this matter in short: anything or object whatsoever, whereby a man, either through the instigation of the devil or his agents, or the corruption of his own heart, or the particular circumstances of his condition, or all of them together, is apt to be drawn or disposed to some sinful action or omission, is that which the Scripture, principally and most properly, calls a temptation."

CHAPTER III.

THE SOURCES OF TEMPTATION.

THE Scripture enumerates three chief sources of temptation,—the world, the flesh, and the devil. These we will consider in succession, though in a different order from that in which they are commonly named.

The First Source of Temptation is Satan, "that Old Serpent, the Devil."

All direct temptation to sin is attributed in Scripture to a malignant spirit, the enemy of God and of all good. The account which the Bible gives of this being is calculated to impress the mind with awe. There is a terrific and horrible grandeur about the prince of hell, as drawn by the pencil of inspiration, which is fitted to excite in us any emotion rather than that of levity. Once seated upon a throne in glory, he has fallen indeed; but still he reigns. He now fills two thrones, instead of one. He reigns over myriads of rebel angels, whom he drew after him into revolt and perdition; and he reigns over a world which he tempted to its ruin.

This archangel fallen, who blighted the bowers of Eden, withered the hope of man, poisoned the cup of human happiness, and opened the door of hell,—is he a plaything, a jest, a bugbear to frighten children? Alas, he never exerts a more damning sway than when his infatuated slaves are disputing about his existence in the study, or tossing his name in profane ribaldry around the midnight bowl!

It is the occupation and the delight of Satan to tempt. He is called, by pre-eminence, *the tempter.* In this employment he has been occupied ever since the day in which he whispered that first fatal lie into the ear of our mother Eve. A spirit,—subtle, piercing, profound,—he has been, during all the vast flow of ages, unceasingly studying our nature in its manifold weaknesses and obliquities. He has tried all sorts of experiments on all sorts of men in all possible circumstances, and has carefully marked the results. He has studied men in societies. He has studied them as individuals. He has studied their powers, their passions, their appetites, and the best modes of assailing their virtue through the play of these various elements of their being.

From the first, the design of Satan, each hour and every moment of each hour, has been the utter and eternal ruin of mankind in hell. A murderer, as well as a liar, from the beginning, of iron will and ever steady to his purpose, he has pursued them, with unwearied tread, through every avenue of existence, thirsting for their blood, and hunting the very life of their soul. Nor has he studied and followed them in vain. Reader! could I but open the door of the pit and uncover its horrors to your gaze, what frightful and overwhelming evidence would you behold of his power to destroy! Appalled by no terrors, hesitating at no wickedness, himself already damned, an agony of living woe, and wrapped about with utter despair, he plays a desperate game. He counts all sin, all crime, all strife, all tumult, all woe, all tears, all destruction as among the most coveted of his victories, the most precious of his gains.

"Tempter," as we have said, is one of the chief titles of this arch fiend. He began his course of temptation but too successfully in paradise; and diligently has he pursued that dark and terrific career ever since. He tempted Cain to kill a gentle and loving brother, and the wretched man imbued his hands in fraternal blood. He tempted Esau to sell his birthright, and a savoury dish was accepted in exchange for the blessing of the first-born. He tempted David to adultery and murder, and prevailed. He tempted Job to curse his day, and triumphed over his integrity. He tempted Peter to deny his Master, and drew him on from denying to cursing and swearing, that he might thereby strengthen his denial. He tempted Judas to betray the Lord of glory, and thirty pieces of silver were received as the price of his blood. He tempted even the pure and blessed Son of God, though to his own discomfiture and dishonour. He is a malicious tempter, intent upon nothing less than the endless ruin of the whole human race. He is a busy tempter, unceasingly lurking for his prey. He is a cunning tempter, full of subtle devices to destroy the souls of men. He is a daring tempter, boldly suggesting crimes of the darkest and most enormous guilt. He is a mighty tempter, as is manifest from those terms of power which the Scripture applies to him, calling him a strong man armed, the god of this world, the prince of the power of the air, the great red dragon, Apollyon (the destroyer,) and other names of might, no less significant.

Satan leads the van in the array of powers hostile to the soul's highest, because eternal welfare. This apostate angel, once the son of the morning, has fallen from the blissful seats of heaven, and now leads the interests of rebellion against Jehovah. He is prince of the infernal powers. He is the god of a rebel world. Every unconverted man is his child, his victim, his slave. And never did eastern despot wield so tyrannical a sceptre, or exact so relentless a servitude.

Saint Paul says of this arch tempter: "We are not ignorant of his devices." Let us contemplate some of these devices, whereby he seeks to lure and destroy the souls of men. They are often framed with matchless skill, and plied with consummate artifice.

When a sinner begins to realize his undone condition and to think seriously of embracing the gospel, this malignant and powerful spirit, the great adversary of souls, instantly takes the alarm; concentrates his strength; calls up the resources of his cunning; and sets himself to oppose and frustrate every effort to escape from his usurped and cruel dominion.

It often happens that his first device is to approach, with shafts of ridicule, the soul that is beginning to ponder the things of its peace. He tries to laugh it out of its serious mood. He jeers it for its scruples and its fears. He calls up its past history to view, and seeks to set its new feelings in a ludicrous contrast. Thus he endeavours to make it ashamed of what he represents as a weak and womanish superstition. Feeble as this artillery is, thousands fall an easy conquest to it. They have been affected under the word. They have been alarmed by sickness. They have been pierced by the arrows of conviction. They have begun to urge the inquiry, "What must I do to be saved?" But by a few well-aimed shafts of profane wit, they are shamed out of their seriousness, and turn back to folly with more ardour than ever.

But this device of the tempter does not always succeed. If conviction has gone deep, it will stand these assaults of ridicule, and still maintain its hold upon the conscience. In that case, the wily foe employs a new device. He pushes his assault with greater vigour. He begins to oppress and harass the soul. He injects blasphemous thoughts. He plies it with baits of sin. He urges it with business. He diverts it with company. He allures it with pleasure. With such weapons of temptation does the adversary often succeed in turning the soul from the narrow way of life, and leading it back to the broad and beaten path, whose end is destruction.

But if these devices, as often happens, fail of their intended effect, the tempter is apt to lay siege to the soul with the cavils of infidelity. Difficulty is made to tread upon the heel of difficulty. Objection after objection starts up to bewilder and affright the anxious inquirer. Doubt upon doubt agitates and distracts the mind. These fiery darts often pierce the soul through and through, and it yields itself an unresisting victim to their assaults.

If these obstacles, however, by prayer and other appropriate means, are removed; if these devices are met and foiled, the cunning tempter again changes his plan of attack. He allows, and even urges, the truth of the gospel. But, with a subtlety truly infernal and diabolical, he makes the very greatness of its blessings an argument with the awakened soul to despair of ever obtaining them. Here, again, his craft is, many times, but too successful; and despair steps in to complete the work, which ridicule, business, company, pleasure, and skeptical doubts had but partially effected.

Thus, with unequalled fertility of resources, does this ever active, ever vigilant, ever cunning tempter vary his ground, as circumstances may seem to require. When foiled in the use of one weapon, he seizes and employs another. He flies from ambush to ambush—he occupies fortress after fortress—he causes one device of wickedness to tread closely upon another—he brings into play, in quick succession, the whole artillery of wit, of flattery, of malice, of skepticism, of despair,—in one word, of temptation in all its Proteus forms and all its malignant power. And, were it not that the soul of the believer is aided and borne forward by an almighty and an all-conquering arm, this malicious and crafty foe, by the variety, the subtlety, and the force of his temptations, would bear down its utmost strength, would foil its wisest skill, would lead it away at last in triumph to the pit, and would bind it there in adamantine and everlasting chains.

The Second Source of Temptation is the World.

What are we to understand by this expression—"the world?" The world, considered as a source of temptation, may be taken in a twofold sense—either as denoting the things of the world, or the men of the world.

In the former of these significations it is used in

the following passages: "If any man love the world, the love of the Father is not in him." "Love not the world, neither the things that are in the world." "They that use this world, as not abusing it." Understood in this sense, the world is a source of temptation, both in the good and the evil that we meet with in it. Honours, preferments, dignities, riches, pleasures, beauty, even meat and drink are temptations. They try us. They bring out and exhibit, both to ourselves and others, what is in us. They often, indeed, prove a snare to us. Though not evil in themselves, they become the occasions of evil by reason of the corrupt affections which they meet in our hearts. So, likewise, the evil things of the world, outward troubles and afflictions,—as perils, losses, poverty, persecution, reproach, calumny, and the death of beloved friends,—are temptations. They try us. They make manifest what we are, both to our own consciousness and to the observation of those around us.

In the latter of the senses named above, the term "world" is used in such passages as the following: "If ye were of the world, the world would love its own." "If the world hate you, ye know that it hated me before it hated you." "We are of God, little children, and the whole world lieth in wickedness." "Ye are of this world; I am not of this world." Here, manifestly, by the world are meant the unregenerate, the wicked, those who refuse Christ, and remain estranged from the spirit and power of his gospel.

Now, it has pleased our Maker, for wise and noble ends, so to constitute the nature of man that he shall be influenced both by the opinion and the example of his fellow-man.

Men are powerfully influenced by the opinion of their fellow-men. This regard to the opinion of others is one of the master-springs of human action. It is one of the main forces that move the whole machinery of human society. Take away from men the love of fame, the desire of approbation, the dread of infamy, the force of emulation, the pride of power, the ambition of wealth, and the passion for display, which are all but modifications of this comprehensive and mighty principle, and the wheels of life are well nigh stopped. Labour languishes; trade droops; learning decays; art loses its object; genius misses its incitement; and society sinks into a repose, dull, stagnant, dreary, and hopeless. This powerful principle, if perverted, becomes dangerous in proportion to its power. Had man continued upright, it would have produced nothing but good; but man has fallen, and it rolls ruin and death through all the ranks of society.

But men are no less powerfully influenced by the example than by the opinion of their fellow-men. One of the most active principles of our nature is that of imitation. Since man was created not to be alone, but to find his happiness and perfection in a social state, and since such a state requires a certain general conformity among the members, the implantation in each of a propensity and an aptitude to assimilate with the rest of the species, is a constitution, in which the wisdom and goodness of the Creator conspicuously appear. If this principle were stricken out of our nature, if men retained all their original diversity of temper, and if that diversity were carried out to its full extent in their actions, society could scarcely exist. Nearness of place, instead of uniting, would but divide men the more. The citizens of the same nation, the inhabitants of the same village, even the members of the same family, would resemble a collection of wild beasts, shut up in the same cage. Endless conflict would ensue in the one case as in the other. The principle of assimilation, of imitation, impressed by the Creator on humanity, is therefore both wise and beneficent. But, like the principle previously noticed, and indeed, like all the principles belonging to human nature, it has been perverted by the fall; and, as in the case of the others, it has become dangerous in proportion to its strength. As this principle, if man had kept his primitive innocence, would have confirmed the loyalty of each by that of all around him, so, since man has fallen, with all the force inherent in it, it draws each into the conspiracy and the wickedness of all the rest. Thus it becomes powerfully active in continuing and spreading the general depravity of the race. There is no man, who has not felt this influence. There is no Christian, who does not acknowledge and deplore it.

What is there, then, in the conduct and example of the world, which is likely to prove hurtful to the interests of the soul? Four things especially, to wit: Its general and habitual forgetfulness of God; its indifference to the gospel of Christ; its low and false standards of morality; and its mistaken estimate and pursuit of happiness.

The World, in general, is habitually Forgetful of God.

The conduct of most men, while unregenerate, is little different from practical atheism. From their conversation God is banished, except when his name is tossed about in thoughtless levity, or introduced to give point to wit or emphasis to anger. In prosperity, there is no recognition of his gifts; in adversity no acknowledgment of his chastening; and in all the varied plans and hopes and fears and successes and disappointments of a busy life, no practical conviction of his providence. When they prosper, they praise their own skill. When they fail, they accuse chance, or blame their fellows. God is not in all their thoughts. Now, as many men of this description have cultivated minds and agreeable manners; as their irreligion takes no obtrusive form, injures in no degree their general standing, nor assails the

Christian doctrine by any open attack; and more especially, as every believer carries a native atheist in his own bosom;—he is in constant danger of being infected by a disease so congenial to his nature, and from which he is himself but in a state of partial recovery. Nothing is more dangerous to a Christian, nothing demands greater watchfulness against its assaults, than this negative iniquity. A denial of his faith would rouse him to combat; open blasphemy would warm him into indignation; but this bodiless, viewless, intangible, unresisting, unfelt, undreaded foe draws him from his principles without touching their truth, and lures him into a forgetfulness of that omnipresence and omniscience, which it essays not to deny.

The World is indifferent to the Gospel of Jesus Christ.

Most men do not openly oppose the gospel. They do not impugn. They do not resist. They do not persecute. They are like Gallio, who "cared for none of these things." Neglect, unconcern, indifference — such are the terms which characterize their feelings and conduct. Whether a particular doctrine is or is not in the Bible, they consider a question, and, indeed, a quarrel, for divines; and who wins or loses is a matter in which they feel little or no concern. They hear the inspiration and divine authority of the Bible questioned, and do not feel that their interest is invaded. It may be true, or it may be false; they have not time to inquire: and if they had, the object would not be worth the pains. Whether a church is revived or declines, whether a mission succeeds or fails, whether the Redeemer's kingdom is enlarged or narrowed in its limits, is, to them, alike indifferent. Now, while surrounded by this chilling indifference, the believer finds it hard to realize the infinite importance of what every body else has heard a thousand times, and yet cares nothing about. Seeing that those around him smile at his zeal, and perchance account him a visionary, he begins to suspect as much himself. He is half inclined, at times, to blush for his singularity. He questions if it be not prudent to check his ardour. Thus, under the notion of guarding against enthusiasm, he is in danger, if, by the grace of God, he do not unceasingly and vigorously stem the opposing current, of sinking into the carelessness and insensibility of "the world that lieth in wickedness," and is dead to God and religion.

The World has Low and False Standards of Morality, and it Acts in Accordance therewith.

The true standard of life and manners, the only standard recognized by Christianity, is the law of God. "Thus saith the Lord," is the principle and the rule of moral obligation. But among the men of the world a very different standard prevails; a standard made up partly of a sentiment of honour, partly of a regard to public opinion, and partly of a dread of human laws.

Honour is the power to which the high-born and the courtly profess to bow. Honour reigns among this class like some feudal monarch emerging from the dust of chivalry, to whose mandate they bow with a prompt and proud submission. At Honour's call they rush to the field of mortal combat. Against all the remonstrances of nature, against all the upbraidings of conscience, against all the yearnings of affection, they deliberately murder their dearest and best loved friend.. A poor man's debt is left unpaid, because it rests only on justice and the law ; but a debt contracted at the gaming table to a man worth his millions, must be paid at every sacrifice, because Honour lifts the voice of command. Call up against that command the authority of God, and the votaries of Honour are prompt to show whose mandate they prefer to obey. They put emphasis into their preference, and glance at the warm blood upon their sword with the greater pride, because it has been shed in disdain and defiance of a narrow religious prejudice.

With a still greater number, the rule of action is the opinion of their neighbours. "What will the world say?" is the question whose answer settles every doubt, and puts an end to all wavering, all hesitation. To escape the censure and win the praise of men is, practically, the end and aim of their morality.

A third class, still more easily resolved, inquire only how they may keep the law of the land. If they can but elude its dreaded grasp, they are content.

In the example resulting from principles and standards of morality, so erroneous and yet so widely embraced, there is, undoubtedly, a strong tempting power. It is true, that from the grossness of the last named principle the Christian finds it no very hard task to keep himself. But to resist the fascination of being esteemed a man of honour, to cleave to the divine law in defiance of the opinion and practice of the world, to keep the conscience free from the usurped dominion of custom, and subject only to its rightful Lord, is a duty by no means of easy performance. Nothing but the grace of God, co-operating with his own watchfulness and diligence, and thus enabling him to resist all adverse influences, will hold the Christian to his loyalty, and keep him, in this regard, "unspotted from the world."

The World is Chargeable with a Mistaken Estimate and Pursuit of Happiness.

What mainly operates to keep men at a distance from God, is the fact that they seek their portion among the things of earth; things temporal and visible; things which the Scripture has named the lust of the flesh, the lust of the eye, and the pride of life. These they esteem good things. These they regard as better suited to content the soul than anything which religion has to offer. These, therefore, they resolve to seek as their supreme good. And through danger, toil, and disappointment, they continue the pursuit. Though they never attain the desired end, they still believe it just before them, and therefore never think of changing their course.

Now, there is a mighty power of temptation in this tide and rush of worldliness, whose sweep is as broad as the circuit of the earth. The Christian is liable to be drawn by it into the world's wrong estimate of good, and the world's wicked conduct resulting from that error. He is liable to be thereby drawn into a conformity with the world in its pride of power and its pride of show; in its avidity of wealth; in its love of pleasure; in its ambition of place; in its thirst of glory; in its spirit of revenge; in its selfishness of affection; in its falsehood and deceit; in its strifes, and envyings, and revilings, and evil speakings; and, indeed, in all its lengthened train of sin and folly.

The young believer, especially, feels, in all its force, the influence of both the principles named above—the power of opinion, and the power of example.

He is surrounded by a great company of rebels against God. The moment he returns to his allegiance he forfeits men's affection in proportion as they are wicked; and he may expect to experience the effect of their resentment. They feel keenly his renunciation of their principles and pleasures.

It is a rebuke which touches both their pride and their conscience. The forms of their ill will, following the bent of their temper and habits, are exceedingly various. The sarcastic leer, the witty remark, the look of pity, the derisive laugh, the lip of scorn, the jocular banter, and the bitter taunt, will, occasionally at least, betray the feelings of hearts, which, under all their pleasantry, are secretly pained and humbled by the new principles and the new life of their former associate.

This hostility sometimes goes to the length of open and relentless persecution; nor are any human ties, however intimate and endearing, a security against its assaults. "A man's foes shall be they of his own household." How often, in the days of bloody persecution, did the nearest relations inform upon each other! How often did fell depravity triumph over the affections of nature, while a parent, a husband, a wife, a sister, or a brother was bleeding under the axe, or consuming in the flame! If these things do not happen to-day, it is not because depravity has changed its nature; but is owing, rather, to the softening and refining, though silent, influence of Christianity itself upon the whole mass of human society, elevating and improving men, even where it fails to impart saving benefits. But the divine sentence still remains true, that "the carnal mind is enmity against God." And think you, reader, that the offence of the cross has ceased? Such a thought is but a dream. The offence of the cross cannot cease, while God hates sin, and sinners hate God.

To this direct hostility of the world, we must add numerous indirect assaults by the same manifold and mighty power of evil. Among these may be enumerated the distractions of business, the bias of interest, the solicitations of pleasure, the allurements of distinction, the charms of power, the love of ease, the gayeties of fashion, and the pressure of continual contact and intercourse with men, whose opinion and example are at war with truth, virtue, and religion. Powerful, almost irresistible, is the force of sympathy and imitation. "Evil communications corrupt good manners." It is irksome and wearying to be always different from those around us. He can have paid but little attention to his own heart, who has not found it hard to maintain the firmness of his own convictions against the current of surrounding sentiment.

These are but a portion of the manifold difficulties, impediments, and hindrances to the Christian life, which combine to make up that formidable enemy, denominated in Scripture the "world;" an enemy scarcely less powerful, scarcely less to be dreaded, than the prince of darkness himself; and opening a fountain of temptation deep, broad, copious, and malignant.

A Third Source of Temptation is the Flesh,—that, is our Carnal and Unsanctified Nature.

Every man, says St. James, is tempted, when he is drawn away of his own lust, and enticed. Satan is a tempter, and the world is a tempter; but their temptations have no such irresistible force as to free us from the responsibility of our evil deeds. The real fountain of temptation, its primal source, is in our own hearts. "The combustible matter (says Henry) is in us, though the flame may be blown up by some outward causes."

The flesh is our greatest enemy. It is a foe within the garrison, always the most dangerous. It is the spring-head of temptation. It is the most effectual of all tempters. It is an open inlet to all the temptations of Satan and the world. It is the very womb in which all sin is conceived, and by which it is brought forth.

The flesh is a hidden and treacherous enemy. When we come home victorious over Satan and the world, we find a traitor within, worse than both. This traitor is that principle of depravity, which inheres in our fallen nature; a principle unlimited in its power of self-multiplication. The evil existing in one human soul, unrestrained, would fill the universe, and involve creation itself in one common ruin. A single sin has filled this world with woe and death. What, then, might not be effected by a depravity whose every pulsation and every acting is sin?

This evil is pent within our bosom. It nestles in every human heart. The conflict with it is the great burden of the Christian's life. Wherever he goes, he carries it with him as a body of death. It dwells in his family. It follows him to his business. It attends him to the sanctuary. It penetrates into his retirement. It poisons his thoughts. It pollutes his imagination. It corrupts his affections. It taints the breath of prayer. It stains the tear of repentance. It debases and deforms all his actions. If we resist the devil, he will flee from us. If we are steady to our principles, the world will at last lose much of its power. But this inward foe is with us every day, and each hour and moment of every day.

CHAPTER IV.

THE STRENGTH OF TEMPTATION.

The Main Power of Temptation, as to its Actual Efficiency over us, lies in our Depravity; that inborn Corruption of Nature, which we have Inherited from our first Parents.

To this original and universal pravity of nature temptation addresses itself. This gives it power to sway the man. Persuasives to sin, strong and commanding, may be addressed to a perfectly holy being. Such persuasives were addressed to our Lord in the desert, and doubtless on many other occasions. But the tempter, as himself informs us, had "nothing in him."

A purity absolutely spotless belonged to his nature. There was no corruption in Christ, nothing sinful, nothing irregular, for the temptation to fasten itself to and work upon; "no tinder (as one has said) for the devil to strike fire into." Consequently the temptation left him unmoved. Persuasion far less powerful, motives far less imperious, are abundantly sufficient, when addressed to beings already inclined to evil, to draw them into transgression. The alloy corrodes at once, while virgin gold remains untouched. The power of temptation is diminished by holiness and increased by sin. So far as a person is unsanctified, he is liable to be overcome by the assaults of temptation; so far as he is sanctified, he is shielded from the fierceness of their power. This fact is at once a strong motive to holy living, and a solemn warning against continuance in sin. Let the believer be encouraged by it to strive after growth in grace. Let the unbeliever be admonished by it to turn back from a path, in which every step of progress only brings him more and more under the power of his enemies. "Temptation finds a man evil, and then makes him worse."

The Power of Temptation is Increased by being addressed to that particular Corruption, that special Form of Transgression, to which a man is peculiarly Prone,—called by the Apostle, our Besetting Sin.

There is not only a general corruption of nature inhering in all men, but there is also, in every man, a special pravity, a particular propensity to some one form of sin, which contracts the general stream of natural corruption into a narrower channel, and gives it a more impetuous flow. "And so advantageous a ground (observes Dr. South) does this afford the tempter to plant his batteries upon, when he would assault us, that he never overlooks it, but observes it exactly, and studies it thoroughly, and will be sure to nick this governing inclination (as I may so express it) with some suitable temptation. So that, whereas by virtue of this some men are naturally choleric and impatient, some proud and ambitious, some lustful, some covetous, some intemperate, some revengeful, and the like; this the devil knows better than any man knows himself. And, accordingly, a man shall be sure to hear from him, and receive many a terrible blow and buffet on his blind side. He is not such a bungler at his art as to use the same nets and baits indifferently for all sorts of game. He will not tempt a shrewd, designing, active, aspiring mind with the gross and low pleasures of wine and women; nor a sot or an epicure with the more refined allurements of power or high place. But, still suiting his proposals to the temper of the person to whom he addresses them, he strikes for the most part home and sure, and it is seldom but he speeds. And, therefore, let a man look to it, and before he enters the combat with so experienced an enemy, who will assuredly find him out, and fight him (if possible) to his disadvantage, let him view and review himself all over, and consider where he lies most opportune and open to a fatal thrust, and be sure to guard himself there, where he is most liable to be mortally struck."

The Deceptive Nature of Temptation greatly increases its Power over us.

All temptation is founded in falsehood, and begins in deceit. To make a man choose evil, you must first persuade him that it is good; for it is against nature to choose evil as such. But when sin has disturbed the judgment, we call evil good, and good evil; we put darkness for light, and light for darkness; we put bitter for sweet, and sweet for bitter. It is, therefore, the uniform tendency of temptation, first to cloud the understanding, and then to beguile and betray the heart. It puts false colours upon things, and cries peace to those who have no true grounds for peace. The great apostacy began in this: "Ye shall not surely die, but shall be as gods." How important, then, that our estimate of things be according to truth! How absurd, how dangerous, the popular dogma, that it is of no consequence what a man believes! Had not Eve *believed* that she would be more happy by eating than by abstaining, the earth had been without a curse, without a prison, without a grave.

The Fact that Temptation always holds out some Advantage, adds immensely to its Strength.

Temptation addresses its solicitations to the love of pleasure, the love of gain, the love of power, the love of fame; in a word, to the love of advantage in some one or other of its many forms. As the fowler scatters seeds upon the ground to lure the silly bird into the snare, so the devil spreads some tempting bait before the sinner to lure him to his ruin. He does not present his poisons undisguised. He offers them under some gilded deceit. He puts a sweetness into the draught of death, that the charmed palate may the more readily swallow the fatal potion. The most venomous serpents abound where the bloom of nature is most luxuriant and inviting. Cleopatra's asp is said to have been brought to her in a basket of flowers. So the fairest delights are often employed by the tempter as vehicles of the grossest sins. The flowers of pleasure offer the deadliest lures. Thus the intemperate are tempted by the sweetness of social joys; the voluptuous by the sweetness of carnal mirth; the covetous by the sweetness of increasing treasures; and the ambitious by the sweetness of clustering honours. To you and to me, reader, Satan offers our peculiar, our dearest joy. He charms and tickles us with delights, that he may lay his strong grasp upon us, and bring us under his iron sceptre. To the sin that easily besets us, our darling sin, the sin to which we are most exposed by our circumstances, our constitution, or our companionship;—to this sin, whatever it may be, he incites us by every provocative which infernal cunning can suggest and infernal malice apply.

The Number and Variety of Occasions to Sin, the Multiplicity of Objects Suited to Allure and Draw us into Transgression, greatly Increase the Vigour and Power of Temptation.

Rain cannot fall except the clouds be charged with vapour; rivers would run dry without the ocean to feed them; fire cannot burn without fuel; in like manner, the strongest inclinations, the most violent passions, the fiercest lusts, would languish and lose their power, if the world afforded no objects to sustain and invigorate them. But such objects are never wanting; on the contrary, they abound on every hand. There are riches for the covetous; honours for the ambitious; and pleasures for the voluptuous. And Satan, as explained in a former paragraph, wisely adapts his assaults to the special bias and propensity which he finds in each individual. He tempts one man to drunkenness; another to sensuality; a third to pride; a fourth to sloth; a fifth to pharisaism;—ever cunningly suiting his baits to the particular bent of whomsoever he may assail.

CHAPTER V.

TEMPTATION TO BE EXPECTED.

As it is pleasant to anticipate good, but irksome to look forward to evil, we are apt to flatter ourselves that, either by our prudence, our strength of resistance, or the special favour of Heaven, we shall escape the terrible trials which befell many of those who have gone before us. But this is a delusion, which will be likely, sooner or later, to yield bitter fruits. Let us glance at the considerations which render it probable that temptation in some form, perhaps in many forms, will assail us in our progress through life.

There is not a Promise in the Bible which assures us against the Assaults of Temptation; on the contrary, the Scriptures tell us, again and again, that Believers must expect to meet with much in this life to Try their Graces of Faith, and Hope, and Courage, and Patience, and so to Test their Fidelity as Christians.

The Christian life is a warfare; an incessant struggle against Satan, against the world, against the flesh; and each under an endless variety of forms. Hence we are exhorted by an apostle to put on the whole armour of God, that we may be able to stand against all wiles and all force. The believer is a pilgrim, a stranger, a sojourner upon the earth. The desert must be trodden. Its burning sands must be encountered. Its parched and arid wastes must be traversed. "In the world ye shall have tribulation," is the Master's legacy to his chosen.

The Character of the Believer is such as to make it certain that he will feel the Assaults of Temptation.

The Christian is sanctified but in part. Many are the remains of indwelling sin even in the holiest. There is no wilder dream than that of a perfect sanctification on earth. David had seen an end of all perfection both in himself and others. There is not a just man on the earth that doeth good and sinneth not. Now, just so far as we are unsanctified, so far are we liable to the solicitations of the world, the flesh, and the devil. Every false principle, every earthly passion, every impure affection, every wicked propensity, every inclination or bias towards evil, is an invitation to the enemy. Nay, it is itself an enemy; restless, active, powerful, ever pushing its subject on to some wicked deed or some sinful indulgence. Ambition, unmortified, is tempted by each dazzling eminence that meets the eye. Covetousness, unsubdued, is excited to a sinful activity by every golden stream that rolls its current at our feet. The fires of envy, pride, anger, revenge, and all other irregular passions, so far as we are unsanctified, will burn and rage under every provocation calculated to fan them into a flame. With such a character, how can we hope to escape the shafts of temptation? Our exposure to these shafts is as wide and as varied as the unparalleled deceitfulness and desperate wickedness of our hearts. If our depravity is dammed up in one direction, it breaks out in another. If checked in its course, the pause only accumulates force for a more terrible rush. As certainly as sin dwelleth in us, so certainly will temptation assail us.

The Circumstances of the Believer are such that he must of Necessity be Exposed to Temptation.

Adversity has its temptations. The poor labourer is apt to envy the lot of those whose wealth enables them to live in ease and luxury. The hungry man finds it hard to take no thought for the morrow. The bereaved can with difficulty make the language of holy Job their own: "The Lord gave, and the Lord hath taken away; blessed be the name of the Lord." To the friendless orphan, who has been cast upon the charities of a cold and selfish world, it is no easy thing to say from the heart: "When my father and my mother forsake me, then the Lord will take me up."

Prosperity has its temptations. Our Saviour sets this fact vividly before us in the declaration that it is as hard for a rich man to enter into the kingdom of heaven as it is for a camel to go through the eye of a needle. The smiles of the world are often harder to be borne in a Christian temper than its frowns. Power tempts to tyranny; greatness, to disdain; riches, to pride and self-indulgence. Moreover, prosperity involves responsibility. *Lay by for charitable uses as the Lord has prospered you,* is the divine standard for benevolent giving. How hard to walk by that rule, when riches increase! To resist the seductions of prosperity requires peculiar grace.

Youth has its temptations. When the blood is warm, when the strength is firm, when the spirits are buoyant, when the world smiles, when all things wear a flattering look, how difficult to realize the emptiness of earth, and to feel the necessity of seeking first the kingdom of heaven!

Middle life has its temptations. The distractions of business, the claims of family, the duties of citizenship, and a thousand other demands upon the time, crowd out all thoughts of eternity, and postpone the great concern to a more fitting opportunity.

Old age has its temptations. The heart still clings to the world; still thinks there is time enough; still repeats its sins in imagination, if not in act; still looks forward to a more convenient season.

Health has its temptations. When the blood flows in a healthful current and we are conscious of entire freedom from disease, then are we apt to imagine that our house stands strong; that we have an inexhaustible supply of energy for expenditure upon the world; and that it will be time enough to prepare for the closing scene, when pain invades our frame, and the trembling limbs give token that the tabernacle of flesh is coming down.

Sickness has its temptations. The sick man is tempted by the pain he suffers, to impatience, to fretfulness, to a rebellious murmuring against God. The suffering of his body tempts him to forget and neglect the interest of his soul. He is tempted to say, or at least to think: How can I repent, how can I pray, how can I seek God, when every thought is, of necessity, absorbed in my anguish, and all my anxieties cluster around my recovery? He is tempted, also, to hope against hope that he will get well again; and this hope is an opiate, which lulls him into a perilous and a fatal security.

The Experience of Believers, in all ages, confirms the truth that they are, and, while in the flesh, ever must be, subject to Temptation.

Where, in all the records of the past, and all the experience of the present, can the saint be found, who has not been called to endure trials?

> "The path of sorrow, and that path alone,
> Leads to the land where sorrow is unknown."

Look at Moses. To what endless trials was he exposed, in the unbelief and murmuring of the people, in the burdens of office, in the envy and opposition of his subordinates, and in the perils, privations, and roughness of his journeyings? Look at

Job. Stripped in a day, of sons, riches, health, friends, honour. Look at Abraham. An exile from his country; a wanderer from land to land; waiting, through years of sickening delay, for the fulfilment of a promise, which was itself contrary to nature; and then called to offer up, in bloody sacrifice, the very child in whom so much fond affection and so many clustering hopes centered. Look at David. Now, destitute, forlorn, and hunted like a partridge upon the mountains; now, softened by the ease and luxuries of royalty, and giving way to a self-indulgence, which had well nigh proved his ruin. Look at the long and illustrious line of patriarchs, prophets, apostles, martyrs, and confessors. They had trial of cruel mockings and scourgings, yea, moreover, of bonds and imprisonments. They were stoned; they were sawn asunder; were tempted; were slain with the sword. They wandered about in sheepskins and goatskins; being destitute, afflicted, tormented. They wandered in deserts, and in mountains, and in dens and caves of the earth.

CHAPTER VI.

TEMPTATION NOT IRRESISTIBLE.

WHILE there are no promises in the Bible against temptation, there are many to cheer and support us under it. Our cross, as well as our crown, is made the subject of divine engagement. One of the most signal and encouraging of these pledges of God's love to us, and of his help in time of need, is found in Paul's first letter to the Corinthians (x. 13): "God is faithful, who will not suffer you to be tempted above that ye are able; but will, with the temptation, also make a way to escape, that ye may be able to bear it."

Sin, as it is an infringement of God's law, is attended with a sense of guilt and a feeling of remorse, often exceedingly distressing. It is not strange, therefore, that man, constituted as he is with an inherent aversion to pain, yet having a strong propensity to sin, should seek to find out some means to keep his conscience quiet under a course of transgression. One of his most common devices to this end is, virtually, to cast the blame of his sins upon God. He looks within, and contemplates the weakness and sinfulness of his own nature; a nature which he claims to have received from God. He looks without, and sees himself surrounded with innumerable temptations; temptations which result from the circumstances in which God's providence has placed him. In this state of things, he flatters himself that he has found, if not a justification, at least an excuse, for his sins; and he secretly exclaims: "What am I, that my Maker should expect me to pursue the path of undeviating rectitude amidst so many influences which are fitted to draw me astray?" With this opiate he puts his conscience to sleep; and, as often as that inward monitor shows signs of awaking, he repeats the soothing application. By this system of consummate trifling with himself, his heart becomes hard as the nether millstone.

The Purpose of the present Chapter is to Expose this Delusion, by Proving that Men are Subject to no Temptations which they are not Able, and of course Under Obligation, to Resist.

This proposition is not, indeed, to be taken without some limitation. Two observations of a qualifying character seem necessary here.

The first is, that man is not, in himself, equal to the mighty achievement here assigned to him. On the contrary, such is his weakness, in a moral point of view, that, if left to his own unaided powers, he will surely fall in any spiritual conflict in which he may engage. It is in the strength of another and higher principle that he is able to triumph,—the principle of grace imparted to him from on high. Though mighty to conquer, the strongest Christian is mighty only through God. So the apostle teaches in the passage before cited. His language is: "God is faithful, who will not suffer you to be tempted above that ye are able." The efficiency, in all successful resistance of temptation, is here taken from the creature and given to the Creator.

The second remark necessary by way of qualification is, that we are not to expect that supernatural grace will be communicated to us independently of our own exertions. God has constituted us moral agents; and he imparts his grace in a manner accordant with the laws of our moral nature. It is, therefore, only when we bring our own faculties into exercise with a view to preservation from ensnaring influences, that we may expect him to work effectually within us to will and to do. God's promise to keep us from falling into temptation, or from falling under temptation, takes for granted that we do our part in endeavouring to avoid it or resist it. If we fail of this, we have no right, from the very condition of the promise, to expect that we shall be preserved. We cannot, with any show of reason, say that he is *not* faithful who has promised, since we ourselves have failed to fulfil the condition on which the promise was made.

To illustrate: A reformed inebriate, who sincerely desires to be a temperate man, but whose appetite for strong drink is yet only partially subdued, ventures into some scene of carousal, where the intoxicating cup is urged upon him, and the cravings of appetite, in connection with what is passing around him, present a temptation which he finds himself unable to overcome, and he falls from his fancied steadfastness into the snare of the devil. Does he say that it was impossible for him to *resist* that temptation? But it was not impossible for him to *avoid* it. He knew, or he ought to have known, that he could not venture on that forbidden ground but at the extremest peril. As he *would* make the mad experiment, he has no cause to marvel at its melancholy issue. And will he now complain that the reason why he fell was, that God did not give him grace to stand? Rather let him humble himself and repent that he has, in this matter, acted the part of a miserable fatalist; that he has voluntarily rushed upon the point of the sword, and then blamed God because he did not miraculously interpose to prevent it from piercing him.

And so it is universally. From the temptations which we court, or to which we needlessly expose ourselves, God has given no pledge, no encouragement even, that he will deliver us. It is only in relation to temptations into which we are involuntarily brought, and which we are unable to shun consistently with the claims of duty, that we have a right to expect his gracious interposition.

Having thus guarded the proposition, that temptation is not irresistible, against misapprehension and misinterpretation, I proceed to confirm and illustrate the truth embodied in it.

The Experience of God's People affords Abundant Proof that Temptation may be Resisted.

If it can be shown that the greatest temptations actually have been resisted, it is surely a rational and a fair conclusion that they are not irresistible.

The influence of custom and example forms one of the most powerful of temptations. But when did this current ever sweep with a broader rush or a more fearful impetuosity than in the time of Noah? He was the only righteous man in the whole world. Yet, with a noble independence, he dared to be singular. Fearlessly, amid scoffs and reproaches, did he stand up and testify for God by a holy profession and a holy life.

The prospect of wealth, and honour, and worldly advancement, has a peculiar fascination, a power of temptation almost unequalled. But Moses declined the distinction of a throne and the riches and luxuries of the regal state, rather than deny his God, sacrifice his religion, or trifle with his conscience.

How strong is the temptation to distrust the goodness and murmur against the providence of God, when the deep waters of affliction roll over the soul, and all we hold most dear is wrested from our grasp! Yet under trials of unparalleled severity,—loss of children, property, health, and friends at one fell blow,—we hear Job declaring: "Though I die, I will not remove my integrity from me." And again: "Though he slay me, yet will I trust in him."

What feeling is there in the human bosom, which, when once aroused, is more violent and unyielding than the passion of revenge? But let the example of David, in his conduct towards Saul, show that there is no temptation in the strongest provocations to this passion, but what may be, by grace, met and overcome.

Is there any principle in man stronger than the love of life? Is there any temptation more powerful than that which is set before a man, who has the alternative of keeping a good conscience or losing his life? Search the records of Christian martyrdom. There you will find the history of multitudes, who marched triumphantly to the stake, and sang songs of victory, while the flames were kindling about them; not because they were insensible to pain, or placed no value upon life; but because their eye pierced the invisible world, and they saw there a glory and a bliss too great to be sacrificed to a momentary exemption from suffering.

The very Nature of Temptation evinces that it is not Irresistible.

Temptation, as we have already seen, properly means trial, experiment, putting a thing to the test. It implies an object to be chosen or refused; some-

5 *

thing to be done or not to be done. The result decides a question which before was doubtful. To suppose that there can be trial in a case where our actions are predetermined in such a sense that we have no control over them, is an absurdity. Temptation necessarily implies liberty of choice between two objects or actions submitted to our election. Where such liberty is not found, temptation is an impossibility.

That Temptation may be Resisted appears from the Nature of Divine Grace.

Grace is given to help our infirmities; to enable us to do what, of ourselves, we are not able to do. But if, after all, it leaves us without the ability to discharge our duty, then, clearly, God's design in communicating it is not accomplished. If it is not grace suited to our necessities, grace that will enable us to triumph over every temptation, it might as well, so far as any useful purpose is answered by it, have been withheld as granted.

That Temptation is not Irresistible is proved from a View of the Moral Constitution of Man.

Man is a moral being, and has all the faculties necessary to intelligent choice. But liberty of choice without a corresponding liberty of action is a self-contradiction. Reason upon the subject as we may, we can never make it plainer than experience makes it to every human being, who but glances at his own mental operations. But the irresistibility of temptation is incompatible with this element of our constitution. It is accordant with no theory of human nature, but that which makes the actions of men subject to the same kind of necessity with that of the brutes.

The Truth of the Proposition that Temptation is not Irresistible is evident from the Destiny as well as from the Character of Man.

What is the great end of man's existence, but to glorify God by conforming to the rule which he hath given? This end, however, he can never attain, if he is subjected to temptations which, in their nature, are irresistible. All other beings fulfil the design of their creation, from the sun that enlightens the world to the flower that blooms on the hill-side; from the bee that labours at the honey, to the seraph that ministers before the throne. And is man alone an exception to this otherwise universal rule? If this be so, vain is his boasted elevation above the brutes. If this be so, his reason, his immortality, can be viewed only as a calamity and a curse.

That no Temptations are Permitted to overtake Men but such as may be Resisted is clear from the Character of God.

God is a being of infinite holiness. And is it consistent with such an attribute to subject his creatures to sin, by an influence, which it is impossible for them to resist?

God is a being of infinite justice. And can this attribute be reconciled with the allegation that he subjects his creatures to the necessity of sinning, and then inflicts upon them the most terrible punishments for yielding to that necessity?

God is a being of infinite truth. And has he not promised that his strength shall be made perfect in our weakness?—that his grace shall be sufficient for us?—that he will not suffer us to be tempted above that we are able to bear? But what becomes of his truth (with reverence be it said), if these promises be not fulfilled? And fulfilled they surely are not, if the doctrine of the resistibility of temptation be not true.

In view, then, of the experience of the church, the nature of temptation, the efficacy of grace, the moral constitution and high destiny of man, and the perfections of God, the conclusion seems to rest upon a solid basis, that no temptation, however violent or long-continued, is, in any proper sense of the term, irresistible, if we betake ourselves to those succours which infinite love and pity have provided.

Some important lessons, of a practical nature, flow from the doctrine, which it has been the object of the present chapter to open and establish.

1. Our Duty in Respect to Temptation is twofold:—partly to Shun it; partly to Resist it.

It is neither possible nor desirable that, in this world, we should avoid all contact with temptation. Herein consists no small part of the discipline by which we are to be fitted for heaven. The general rule of duty on this subject seems to be this: never, on the one hand, to expose ourselves to temptation needlessly, and especially not for the sake of showing our ability to withstand it; and never, on the other hand, to decline encountering it by turning our back upon duty. When we meet temptation in the former case, we have every reason to anticipate defeat; when we encounter it in the latter, we have every reason to hope that, trusting in God's grace, we shall be preserved from falling under its power.

2. There is not a more Alarming Indication in the Character of a Professing Christian than a Spirit of Self-confidence.

What a solemn warning against the indulgence of such a spirit is given to us in the fall of Peter! Peter was sincere in his passionate protestations of friendship and fidelity to the Saviour. He verily believed that he would die with his Master rather than deny him. The world knows the sad issue. The secret of it all was (as it is in every case in which the Christian is left to fall), that he trusted in his own strength. And what, upon this subject, is the sentence of inspired wisdom? This: "He that trusteth in his own heart is a fool." And the same divine wisdom, through the pen of Jeremiah, tells us why. It is because "the heart is deceitful above all things, and desperately wicked."

3. The Spirit of the Gospel is a Spirit of Compassion and Kindness towards those who have Fallen before the Power of Temptation.

While we look upon the conduct of such with disapprobation, we are but too apt to load them with reproaches, and to turn despairingly, if not scornfully, away from them, as if their case were utterly hopeless. But are we sure that we have formed a proper estimate of their condition? Are we sure that we have any just idea of the nature and strength of the temptation to which they yielded? Are we sure that, with all our fancied power of resistance, we might not, in similar circumstances, have fallen in the same manner, and possibly more deeply than they? Ought we not, then, rather to give thanks to God for having held us up, than to deal out severe censures upon them, in consideration of their having been left to fall through the power of the adversary? And certainly we have no right to look upon them with disdain, so long as we ourselves are subject to the infirmities of the flesh, nor to regard their case as hopeless, so long as the grace of God remains omnipotent.

4. Finally: If we would Resist Temptation Without, we must Crucify Corruption Within.

If there were within us no predisposition to yield to temptation, we should be comparatively secure. When the devil assaulted our blessed Lord, he found "nothing in him" to favour the onset. We, on the contrary, are always exposed, always insecure, because we have corrupt propensities, which incline us, not to resist, but to yield to temptation. Reader, would you live in comparative security in this tempting world? Would you pass through its temptations in the character of a conqueror? Then slay your inward foes. Resist the motions of unsanctified affection. Aim to bring every thought into captivity to the obedience of Christ. Do this, and you will, in great measure, disarm and destroy the power of outward temptations. Do this, and you will win and wear the honours of a spiritual victory more glorious than the proudest of earth's conquests. Do this, and, with a serene and holy courage, you may

"Smile at Satan's rage,
And face a frowning world."

CHAPTER VII.

THE REFUGE OF THE TEMPTED.

OUR refuge from the tempter, our strength against his temptations, is next to be considered. This is expressed in one word—Christ. Satan fears no other power. Our fastings, our penances, our mortifications, our resolutions, our vows, our self-tortures, our covenants written in blood, our oaths to God, and all our succours and assistances from human power he scorns and derides. But Christ is Lord over this son of pride. In Christ's strength the weakest believer is impregnable as the towers and battlements of heaven itself. The life-long lesson of a Christian is, to oppose Christ's might to Satan's power, Christ's wisdom to Satan's wiles, Christ's righteousness to Satan's accusations.

But how are we to obtain the needed succours from our Divine and Almighty Helper? The principle in which we are to resist, the power by which we are to overcome, is faith. "Whom resist," says an apostle, "steadfast in the faith." Again: "Fight the good fight of faith." Still again: "This is the victory that overcometh the world, even your faith." Faith, a warm, living, earnest trust in Christ, is the weapon to be employed against all our spiritual enemies.

Faith is the weapon by which we overcome the world. The world tries both to allure and to terrify. It labours at once to beguile and to alarm. And how do we conquer this busy and powerful foe? Faith is the victory that overcometh. Faith recognizes the world as an enemy's country. Faith lifts the Christian above the world. Faith looks to the better land. Faith sings: "This is not my rest, for it is polluted."

"I seek a country out of sight,
A city in the skies."

Faith is the weapon by which we overcome the flesh. "Flesh is a dangerous foe to grace." The unsanctified nature looks at present good, desires present gratification, rests in present contentments. "Faith is the substance of things hoped for, the evidence of things not seen." It apprehends eternal verities. It realizes the invisible. It brings distant and unseen things near, and makes them seem like present and visible realities. Faith crucifies the flesh; mortifies the deeds of the body; applies to the Great Physician; brings into the soul the cleansing balm; confesses sin, and obtains forgiveness.

Faith is the weapon by which we overcome the

devil. The great adversary tempts and harasses the soul; but faith holds fast to the Divine word. Satan says: "God has forsaken you." Faith replies: "God has promised, 'I will never leave thee nor forsake thee.'" Satan says: "You will not hold out—you will fail to persevere." Faith replies: "God has said, 'As thy day is, so shall thy strength be;' God's grace is sufficient; Divine strength shall be given." Satan says: "You will perish after all." Faith replies: "Christ's promise runs—'My sheep shall never perish.'" Thus faith is the shield by which we quench all the fiery darts of the devil.

That faith is the principle on which we shall successfully contend against the assaults of the tempter, appears from an observation previously made, that temptation is evermore founded in deceit. Faith embraces the Divine testimony, and cannot be deceived. Satan may sing in our ears as long as he will, that sin is a pleasant thing; he sings in vain, while the soul believes the Divine declaration, that "sin is an evil and bitter thing," and that "the way of the trangressor is hard." Satan may exert his utmost art to persuade us that it is a mean, spiritless, gloomy thing to serve God; it is all to no purpose, as long as the soul is acting faith in the Divine testimony that God's service is excellent and glorious. Faith brings the soul to Christ; assures it of his grace; convinces it of his power; and hides it under the shadow of his arm.

So much faith as a Christian has in exercise, so much spiritual strength does he possess. Our perseverance itself, though secured in heaven, is dependent on the continuance of our faith. When our gracious Lord showed Peter his danger and assured him of final deliverance, he told him: "I have prayed for thee, that thy faith fail not." And all believers are declared in the Divine word to be such as are "kept by the power of God through faith unto salvation."

Could faith utterly fail, Satan would gain a complete and final conquest. But while this grace remains, as by covenant it shall remain in all true believers, though he may gain victories, he shall never conquer. Faith rises, like Antæus, from the ground, and seems at times, as in the case of Peter, to have gained fresh strength by the fall. It renews the combat once and a thousand times. Thus shall it struggle on even to the end; and, at last, bear its possessor triumphant over all foes, all fears, all clouds, all storms, all sorrows; yea, over death itself.

CHAPTER VIII.

ENDURING TEMPTATION.

The apostle James pronounces a benediction upon the man that "endureth temptation." How is this blessing to be obtained? In other words, what is it to endure temptation?

It is necessary to bear in mind, here, the strict meaning of the term as denoting trial, and the fact that it is used in a good as well as a bad sense. Sometimes, and indeed generally, as the word is used in Scripture, temptation signifies a direct and positive enticement tó sin. In this sense, temptation never comes directly from God. Not unfrequently, however, the word signifies a providential arrangement, by which God makes trial of a man, to bring out and render evident what is in him. Thus God raises one man to place and power, that it may be seen whether he will remain humble in his exaltation. He makes another rich, that it may be seen whether he will open his hand to the poor. He keeps a third poor, that it may be seen whether he will bear his affliction without murmuring. He brings a fourth into sickness, that it may be seen whether he will be patient under pain and languor. And so in regard to innumerable other trials. Such we know to have been the object of the terrible trials, to which holy Job was subjected; from the circumstances attending those trials as related in Scripture, and particularly from the Lord's address to Satan: "Hast thou considered my servant Job, that there is none like him in the earth, a perfect and an upright man, one that feareth God, and escheweth evil?" Even direct motions and enticements to sin never occur without providential permission. So that, at last, all temptations, come from whatever quarter they may, are of the nature of trials, and their design and issue is to prove and make manifest what is in man.

Now, to endure temptation is, certainly, not to run into it, as Balaam and Saul did. Neither is it simply to meet it, as Moses did in the wilderness, on descending from the Mount, after receiving the tables of the law. Nor yet is it to resist, however resolutely, for once or twice, assaults upon our faith and virtue.

To endure temptation, in the sense of the apostle, is to bear up, with Christian fortitude, under all trials, and to resist, with Christian courage, all the assaults of Satan and of sin.

It is to hold fast our integrity, even though the trial require us to descend into the lions' den, or walk through the fiery furnace; nay, though it calls us to cut off a right hand, or pluck out a right eye. It is to stand in our temptation, whatever it may be; for there is no man, whom God does not try, in one way or another,—either efficiently or permissively; that is, by the direct arrangements of his providence, or by withholding his grace, which he is under no obligation to bestow, and so letting Satan and other spiritual enemies exert, up to a certain limit, their forces upon him. The man who endures temptation is, in the words of Cecil, the one who "weathers it. He expects it; and, when it comes on him, he is not surprised. He knows that it is impossible to give place to it, in any degree, with safety. He resolves, therefore, by the help of God, to make a stand. Though the current may run strong against him, he knows certainly, that he must either go against the current, or be carried away, and perish for ever."

CHAPTER IX.

THE AGENCIES WHEREBY TEMPTATION IS TO BE ENDURED.

The First Source of Strength in Bearing up under the Trials we meet, and the Temptations which assail us, is, to be Sensible of our own Weakness.

It ought to be deeply impressed upon our mind, and habitually present to our thought, that we are not sufficient of ourselves to withstand any temptation. When Bunyan saw a convict passing the window on his way to the gallows, he exclaimed: "There, but for the grace of God, goes John Bunyan." It is true that, through Christ strengthening us, we can do all things; but it is no less true that, without Christ strengthening us, we can do nothing. Our true wisdom, therefore, is to distrust ourselves. When we are weak, then are we strong. This is a paradox to the world; but not to the Christian. When most conscious of our own weakness, we are most apt to have recourse to a better strength. Then we are strong, not in ourselves, but in the grace which is in Christ Jesus. Then we betake ourselves to the SOURCE of all our ability, even the aids afforded by Christ, through the Holy Spirit.

The more we are brought down in our estimates of our own strength, the more do we experience the supports of divine strength.

We are wholly insufficient, of ourselves, to meet the feeblest assaults of our enemies. What can a child of the dust do against the policy and power of angelic natures, though fallen? What can a being, made to be swayed by the opinion and example of his fellow-creatures, do against the combined belief and practice of the world? But, above all, what can depravity do against itself? Can death produce life? Can enmity turn itself into love? Can pollution beget purity?

A Second Source of Strength in Enduring or Resisting Temptation is to Know and Feel the All-sufficiency of God; to be sensible of his Sovereign Power against all adverse Powers; and to have Recourse to it, either to keep us from Temptation, or to keep us in Temptation.

When the number, craft, and power of our enemies are considered, it is most manifest that a strength superior to our own is necessary to turn back the battle from the gate, and to give us the victory over Satan, the world, and the flesh. This is a work for the arm of omnipotence. When done at all, it must be done by him, who "was manifested to destroy the works of the devil." It must be done by him, who hath "overcome the world." It must be done by him, who "saves his people from their sins."

The instrument by which the Divine strength is realized, the agency whereby it is brought to our aid and made effective for our support, is, as has been already stated in a former chapter, faith. It is those who are steadfast in the faith, that are enabled to resist the devil. It is, in like manner, those who have faith, that overcome the world. It is, again, equally those who possess this precious grace, that have power to subdue the lusts of the flesh, since "faith works by love and purifies the heart." Reader, believe the Divine strength. Trust in it firmly. Doubt not that it is able to subdue both your external and internal foes. Cast yourself unreservedly upon its promised aid. Do all this from the heart; and rest assured, that the mighty God will strengthen you against the might of all your enemies.

To be Sensible of the Dangers that Beset us, is Indispensable to our Escape from them.

We live in the midst of enemies. Satan and his legions plot against us; and our own corruptions are in traitorous correspondence with them. Alas, their snares are laid for us in all our ways! There is no place, there is no condition, that is not full of them. They invade our solitude. They pursue us in public. They stay not even from our devotions. Satan is expressly compared to a fowler, whose occupation it is to set gins and snares for the silly birds. As the fowler covers up his trap, so do the devil and the world conceal the baits by which they would lure us to sin. As the fowler adapts his enticements to the nature and habits of the bird which he seeks to catch, so do our spiritual enemies suit their solicitations to our special tastes and propensities. As the fowler tempts the bird with the seeds scattered upon the ground, so does Satan tempt the carnal heart with the sweetness of sinful gratifications. As the fowler oft employs variety of snares to compass the ruin of the same bird, so Satan not unfrequently assaults the soul with divers temptations, and leaves no means unemployed, no stone unturned, to effect its destruction.

> "The close pursuer's busy hands do plant
> Snares in thy substance; snares attend thy want;
> Snares in thy credit; snares in thy disgrace;
> Snares in thy high estate; snares in thy base;
> Snares tuck thy bed; and snares attend thy board;
> Snares watch thy thoughts; and snares attach thy word;
> Snares in thy quiet; snares in thy commotion;
> Snares in thy diet; snares in thy devotion;
> Snares lurk in thy resolves; snares in thy doubt;
> Snares lie within thy heart; and snares without;
> Snares are above thy head; and snares beneath;
> Snares in thy sickness; snares are in thy death."

And shall we sleep secure, amid foes that never sleep? Amid perils so numerous and so manifold, not to be sensible of their existence and ever on our guard against them, is to tempt God and court our own destruction.

If we would be Able to Endure or Resist Temptation, we must be Careful to Avoid Temptation, whenever it can be done without Deserting or Neglecting Duty.

They who rush unnecessarily into temptation, cannot reasonably expect to come out of it unharmed. The promise of assistance is to those only who endure it, who resist it, who struggle against it; not to those who invite it. We are never, of choice, to expose ourselves to any temptation. But when, in the providence of God, without our seeking and against our choice, we fall into temptation, then our plain duty is to meet it resolutely, looking to God for special aid, which, agreeably to his promise, will certainly, in all such cases, be graciously afforded.

Another Rule for Enduring Temptation is, when Temptation Assails, to Resist it at once, with Determined Resolution and Effort.

Only by pursuing this method can we have any rational prospect of withstanding the assault ultimately. All dallying with temptation is both sinful in itself and dangerous in its tendency. Indeed, it is almost sure to end in compliance. It is apt to provoke God to withhold or withdraw that gracious influence, without which we are sure to fall. Christ, by teaching us to pray that we may not be led into temptation, warns us to distrust ourselves. Temptation, it is true, is not necessarily followed by sin; but it is, nevertheless, very apt to be. He who carries inflammable materials about him, should keep at a distance from the fire. Many a fair character, both in the world and the church, if led into temptation, would be soon stripped of his glory. A man who is going down hill cannot always stop when he would. So he who, trusting to the strength of his resolution, tampers with dangerous occasions, will be apt to find himself often carried beyond his purpose. Therefore the only safe rule is, to resist the beginnings, to struggle against the first assault.

The Frequent Re-union and Intimate Converse of the Saints is an Excellent Means of Resisting Temptation.

"Then they that feared the Lord," says the prophet Malachi, "spake often one to another." And the exhortation of St. Paul to the Christians of his day was: "Forsake not the assembling of yourselves together." Did Christians close their ranks, they would strengthen each other's hands, and greatly lessen the common danger. But, by keeping aloof from each other, and engaging their enemies, as it were, single-handed, they give them every possible advantage, and must feel the evil consequence in the weakening of their strength by the way.

A Deep and Abiding Sense of the Divine Presence is a Shield against Temptation.

God's eye is upon all actions and all thoughts. It is so piercing that no wickedness can be hid from him. It is so pure that none can be seen without abhorrence. The darkness and the light are both alike to him. Midnight is as noonday. We cannot steal a thought out of his sight, though it be sudden and rapid as the lightning; "for in him we live, and move, and have our being." We can no more be removed from the presence of God, than we can be removed from ourselves. We are encompassed by his essence; wrapped up, as it were, in the bosom of his infinite nature. "The consideration of this great truth (says Jeremy Taylor) is of a very universal use in the whole course of the life of a Christian. All the consequences and effects of it are universal. He that remembers that God stands a witness and a judge, beholding every secrecy, besides his impiety, must have put on impudence, if he be not much restrained in his temptation to sin. For the greatest part of sin is taken away, if a man have a witness of his conversation; and he is a great despiser of God, who sends a boy away when he is going to commit fornication, and yet will dare to do it, though he knows God is present, and cannot be sent off; as if the eye of a little boy were more awful than the all-seeing eye of God. He is to be feared in public, he is to be feared in private: if you go forth, he spies you; if you go in, he sees you; when you light the candle, he observes you; when you put it out, then also God marks you. Be sure that while you are in his sight you behave yourself as becomes so holy a presence. But if you will sin, retire yourself wisely, and go where God cannot see: for no where else can you be safe. And, certainly, if men would always actually consider, and really esteem this truth, that God is the great eye of the world, always watching over our actions, and an ever open ear to hear all our words, and an unwearied arm ever lifted up to crush a sinner into ruin, it would be the readiest way in the world to make sin to cease from amongst the children of men, and for men to approach to the blessed estate of the saints in heaven, who cannot sin, for they always walk in the presence, and behold the face of God."

Another Excellent Means of Enduring or Resisting Temptation, is to get the Relish of Spiritual Delights deeply Seated in the Soul.

Who would leave royal dainties to feed on husks? So a heart in heaven, a heart in love with spiritual pleasures, will not stoop to play with the baits of sin. It was upon this principle that Christ himself, our great example and model, endured temptation. Of him it is declared, that "for the joy that was set before him," the infinite and everlasting delights of heaven held out to him in prospect as the reward of his mediatorial work, "he endured the cross, despising the shame." And shall not that, which was a source of strength to the Master, be also a power of resistance to his followers?

Looking unto Jesus is a still further Means of Resisting Temptation.

This is the apostle's rule. "Let us (he says) run with patience the race set before us, looking unto Jesus." Looking unto Jesus means acting faith on him. Another apostle says: "This is the victory that overcometh the world, even your faith." Faith takes hold of the strength of Jesus, which is made perfect in our weakness. Faith leans upon him as the Rock of Ages. Faith reposes on him as our helper in every trial. Faith looks up to him as our leader in the contest. Faith stimulates and helps us to imitate his example. He endured the assaults of Satan. He endured the contradiction of sinners against himself. Nay, he endured the cross itself, despising the shame, and triumphing over the anguish. And they who look unto him, in the sense of the apostle, realize his strength, and shall renew his victories.

Hope is another Principle of Spiritual Strength in the Hour of Temptation.

"Which hope we have (says St. Paul) as an anchor of the soul." The office of an anchor is well known. The sailor, when his ship is tossed with fierce winds, and he fears that she will be driven upon rocks and dashed in pieces, throws out his anchor, and holds fast by its bite; and so the vessel is enabled to weather the storm. Such, according to the apostle, is the blessed office of hope. We have it, he says, as an anchor of the soul. Of course, it has a spiritual function of the highest importance, even that of enabling us to stand up against the rage of Satan, the fascinations of the world, and the enticements of our own corrupt nature.

David made use of the anchor of hope, even when the storm of temptation was at its height, when it raged to such a degree that men spake of stoning him. "He encouraged himself in the

Lord his God." Hope was his anchor. By it he was enabled to endure. Upon another occasion of deep distress, we see him using the same remedy. "Why art thou cast down, O my soul? Why art thou disquieted within me? Hope thou in God." This was the anchor which he dropped amid the raging billows, and by it he rode securely till the storm was past.

Job, too, endured on this principle. When he could see God neither on the right hand nor the left, he still hoped on. He declared his confidence that, when God had tried him, he should come forth as gold. It was a severe trial, and he was called to weather it in the dark. But, by using hope as an anchor, he came out of it unharmed.

We also are called to endure trial. The waves of temptation will beat. Storms will come. We must expect to encounter rough weather on our voyage. But God has given us an anchor: "which hope we have as an anchor of the soul."

Another Principle of Resistance to Temptation, and Endurance under it, is Love to Christ.

This love, "shed abroad in the heart," is stronger than death; else there had never been a martyr. If, then, we would successfully struggle against the temptations that assail us, if we would bear up manfully against the trials of life, we must grow in the love of Christ. As the love of Christ increases, the love of sin and all inferior things decreases. This divine affection consumes all opposing affections. It is a bundle of myrrh, which has power to preserve the soul from all its corruptions.

Vigilance is a most Necessary and Effective Agency for Resisting Temptation.

On this point we have the mind of the Great Teacher. The rule here laid down is one given by himself. His language is: "Watch and pray, that ye enter not into temptation."

By watchfulness is to be understood that state of the soul in which it is carefully attentive to its own condition, observes with anxiety its own exercises, scrutinizes the actings of external things upon itself, and has a present persuasion of the dangers which threaten, and the grace which can alone preserve and sustain it.

In a world like this, subject to the sway of our greatest enemy, we may expect the worst of evils, unless we watch against their approach. He who knows what is in man has said: "What I say unto you I say unto all, Watch." Let us, then, by earnest attention to our own heart, first endeavour to discover where our weakness lies, and then vigilantly guard against whatever addresses itself to our besetting corruptions. Our foes are quick-sighted, alert, skilful, resolute, and persevering. They understand how to take advantage of time, place, and circumstance. They know both when to retire and hide themselves till the soul is lulled into a treacherous security, and when to rush suddenly upon it and take it captive before it has time for thought or resistance. They know how to entice its desires, how to quell its apprehensions, how to deaden its spiritual affections, how to inflate its false confidences, and how to oppress it with groundless and unbelieving fears. The watchful Christian will learn to anticipate their approach, and to guard against their assaults. This watchfulness will greatly increase his knowledge of the craft and power of Satan, of the strength and malignity of sin, of the grace and faithfulness of Christ, and of the emptiness of the world and the blessedness of heaven. In a word, it will help the believer's growth in every Christian grace, and will send warmth and vigour along every artery of the Christian life.

Prayer is the Last and the Most Powerful Agency for Resisting or Enduring Temptation.

These two agencies, vigilance and prayer, so directly and strongly recommended by our Saviour himself, continually re-act upon each other. They are reciprocal and inseparable. He who watches will pray, and he who prays will watch.

Prayer is needful at all times; for we are always weak, always short-sighted, always in want. Our heart is like a vessel full of holes, which nothing can keep full but a constant stream. The new man of the heart is a creature; and, like other creatures, it must receive daily nutriment, or it dies. A believer must obtain continual supplies of grace from Christ, or his spiritual life will wither and decay; and prayer is the channel through which these supplies must come.

But prayer is ever most needful when it is most difficult. When all goes well, it is easy and pleasant to come to our Elder Brother for the blessings of grace. But when the foe approaches, when temptation assails, when corruption is active, when guilt clouds the conscience, when the light of heaven is withdrawn and the storm begins to descend, then it is that we most need to come near our shelter. But then, alas! precisely then,—such is our perverseness,—we are apt to invent a thousand reasons why we may not and cannot draw nigh. This is the masterpiece of hell—first to bring the soul into straits, and then to persuade it that the very circumstances which create its danger should keep it back from its only refuge.

But now how beautiful does the grace of our loving Redeemer appear! His tender regard is toward the believing soul, notwithstanding its folly. He gently holds it up. He graciously brings it, in despite of its doubts and fears, to the foot of his throne, there to utter its plaintive cry. That cry, trembling believer, faint and feeble though it be, has still power to pierce the heavens. It is heard by Him whose habitation is in the excellent glory. "For the oppression of the poor, for the sighing of the needy, now will I arise, saith Jehovah." And as our Redeemer arises, hell retires.

How much less should we sin, how much less should we suffer, did we but continue steadfast and resolute in prayer, when most we need the succour, thence and thence alone to be obtained! The conflict even then might be severe, but it would be short; and the end would be crowned with victory, and full of glory.

CHAPTER X.

HOPE UNDER TEMPTATION.

We are next to consider the grounds of encouragement, hope, and consolation, which remain to the child of God, even under the sorest temptations. These are neither few nor small.

The First Ground of Encouragement under Temptation is, that these Trials, which so Weary and Distress the Spirit, are far from being any Indication that God has rejected a Man.

Quite the reverse of this is the truth. The very anguish which they occasion is a presumptive proof that there is saving grace in the soul. It is evidence of the struggle within, noticed by Paul in the Romans, between the law in the members and the law of the mind; between the old man and the new; between nature and grace. Let tempted souls remember that the most eminent saints,—Joseph, Moses, Job, David, Jeremiah, Paul, Luther, and an infinite series of the holiest men,—have known most of Satan's enmity; have felt the utmost efforts of his rage. Courage, then, tempted believer! These are the footsteps of the flock. When was God's own Son, the man Christ Jesus, dearer to the Father, than when the storm raged most violently, and beat most fiercely upon him? Should it be otherwise with thee?

A Second Ground of Encouragement is, that Temptation Resisted is a Source of Strength.

The law of exercise is of universal application, extending from the energy of a muscle to the highest intellectual and moral faculties. The strength of the body and the powers of the soul are developed, invigorated, and brought to their proper maturity, by use. Grace forms no exception to this rule. Like every other power in man, it grows and strengthens through exercise. Every assault of the devil, repelled and overcome, increases our spiritual might. Habits are formed by a constant repetition of the same acts. The habit of resisting evil follows this law. And who is ignorant of the power of habit? It seems clothed with a species of omnipotence. How important that gracious habits should be formed and matured in the soul! But this can be effected only through trials. Thus patience is the fruit of frequent acts of submission to afflictive providences. Hope attains its full strength only through repeated actings under circumstances similar to those so vividly described by David in the 42d and 43d Psalms, wherein, from the depths of his distress, we hear him, again and again, exclaiming: "Why art thou cast down, O my soul? and why art thou disquieted in me? hope thou in God: for I shall yet praise him for the help of his countenance." Faith reaches a manly maturity and vigour only by often acting confidence in God, under circumstances in which human help is impotent and unavailing; as in the case of David again, when the people became so enraged as to speak of stoning him, whereupon, according to the record, "David encouraged himself in the Lord his God." The case is similar in respect to all other graces. So that, in effect, trials endured, temptations resisted and conquered, are a fountain of spiritual strength, a precious means of growth in grace. And is there not comfort to tempted souls in such a fact?

A Third Ground of Consolation and Hope in Trial is, that the Fiercest Temptations, whether of Satan, the World, or the Flesh, being Overcome, are, in the Issue, exceedingly Glorious to Him whom the Christian delights to Honour.

In nothing do the sovereignty, wisdom, power, and faithfulness of the Redeemer appear more conspicuous, than in supporting his saints under temptation and giving them the victory over it. The tenderness of his compassion, the condescension of his love, the long-suffering of his grace, all those amiable perfections which are the charm and the joy of heaven, here blend their softened rays, and shine with united splendour. The Redeemer receives more glory in bringing one tempted soul to heaven, than in preserving a universe of spirits that never sinned. In this he shows that he is not only able to vanquish the powers of hell himself, but that he can impart strength to a worm to achieve the same victory.

The Assurance that Trials convey Precious Lessons is another Ground of Encouragement while we are passing through them.

As through a series of difficulties a person gains a knowledge of the world, and by a succession of campaigns a soldier is instructed in the art of war, so by enduring temptation a believer increases in spiritual wisdom. Solomon says, that "it is better to go to the house of mourning, than to the house of feasting." Why? He immediately adds the reason: "for that is the end of all men, and the living will lay it to his heart." Thus we see that the house of mourning affords us an excellent lesson. It impresses upon us the nearness and certainty of our end. It brings us to a recollection and thoughtful consideration of that momentous fact. It seals the lesson upon our heart; induces sobriety; and prompts the solemn self-inquiry, "What shall I do in the end thereof?"

But if a mere going to the house of mourning is so fruitful of salutary instruction, what may we not expect, in this regard, from being ourselves dwellers in that house? The lessons thus imparted must be more effectual, as well as more impressive. Accordingly, David relates this experience in his own case: "Before I was afflicted, I went astray; but now have I learned thy word." And again, to the same effect: "It is good for me that I have been afflicted, that I might learn thy statutes."

Luther, commenting on this experience of the Psalmist, adds a declaration of his own: "I never knew the meaning of God's word, till I was afflicted." Affliction stops a man in his course; arrests and fixes his thoughts; and, when sanctified, quickens his spiritual vision.

The Divine word assures us that God alone is our portion: affliction brings into our consciousness a realization of that vital truth. The word tells us that sin is an evil and a bitter thing: affliction causes us to taste its bitterness. The word enjoins prayer: affliction brings us to our knees. The word teaches us that we are members one of another: affliction stirs our sympathetic emotions, and makes us Christ-like in temper, who (the apostle tells us) was therefore tempted, that he might know how to succour them that are tempted. It is thus that temptation teaches. It is thus that it reinforces God's word. It is thus that it imparts the best lessons, and imparts them in the most effective way.

Nothing teaches like experience. Temptation imparts an interest to religious truth and duty, unknown and unfelt without it. By it, a man is disciplined into an acquaintance with his Saviour, whom he therefore trusts and loves the more. By it, he is disciplined into an acquaintance with Satan, whose wiles he thereby learns the more successfully to foil. By it, he is disciplined into an acquaintance with the world, whose assaults he is thus enabled the more skilfully and vigorously to resist. By it, he is disciplined into an acquaintance with himself, so that he is led to distrust his own strength, and to look to a higher power for ability to overcome the motions of indwelling sin. The result of all is, that he comes to be less easily deceived, and so escapes the loss and the anguish which former lapses occasioned.

Affliction, as before intimated, teaches and enforces the lesson of prayer. But prayer brings us direct supplies from heaven. It overawes the adversary. It weakens the power of the world. It sheds a withering influence over all our own corruptions.

Moreover, affliction, when sanctified, begets an appetite for the word. But a diligent attendance upon the word, with a careful recollection and seasonable application of it, cuts the sinews of Satan's temptations; counteracts the false maxims and evil examples of the world; and affords unspeakable assistance in fathoming the depths of our own hearts, and in repelling and subduing the ever-springing evils which have their seat and source within.

A still further Encouragement and Support under Temptation, is that the Anguish arising from the Sorest Trials will but make the Soul's Rest in God more Sweet and Precious.

Is the harbour welcome to the sailor, long tossed upon the deep? And is it not all the more welcome for the storm? Is home a gladdening sight to the traveller after a perilous journey? And is it not all the more gladdening because of the dangers past? So shall heaven be to thee, thou tossed with tempest and not comforted. Look forward and upward! The glorious vision already skirts the horizon. A few more toils endured, a few more perils past, shall bring thee to thy home. There thou shalt meet a thousand shining saints, once in the furnace like thyself. The tempted mourner of Uz is there, no more to seek the refuge of the grave. The tempted disciple of Bethsaida is there, never again to deny the Master whom he loves. The tempted martyr is there, to tell thee how welcome Christ can make the fagot and the flame. But what do I say? The tempted Son of God is there, to wipe the latest tear from thy eye, and welcome thee to that rest which remaineth for the people of God.

It is an Inexhaustible Fountain of Consolation and Encouragement to the Believer under his Trials, to know that his Immortal Life is Secure.

"I give unto my sheep eternal life," said the Master to his disciples, "and they shall never perish." Believers are bought by Christ. They are the purchase of his groans and anguish, of his tears and blood. And will he part with his own?

God has promised eternal life to as many as have been redeemed by Christ. And "God's promises are bonds that never yet were dishonoured. If he hath said he will, he will." (*Spurgeon.*)

Christ has pledged his oath that he will present to the Father all whom he has purchased by his cross. He is the divine sponsor for all his chosen. His word to the Father is: "At my hand shalt thou require them." That oath shall never be vacated. The truth and honour of the Redeemer are involved in its fulfilment to the last tittle.

Believers are united unto Christ. His Holy Spirit, like a common soul, animates them all. And will he cut off a part of himself?—those whom his inspired apostle has declared to be "members of his body, of his flesh, and of his bones?" No, my Christian brother, your Lord has many saints; but he has not one to lose.

It is an Unspeakable Encouragement to Believers under Trial to know that their "Light Afflictions, which are but for a moment, shall work out for them a far more Exceeding and Eternal Weight of Glory."

St. James says of such, that when they are tried, that is, approved, they "shall receive the crown of life." There is a crown of ambition, for which men have waded through seas of blood. There is a crown of fame, for which men have toiled at the midnight lamp till health and life gave way. There is a crown of wealth, for which men have sacrificed conscience and character, as well as ease and quiet. There is a crown of roses, for which men have been willing to give up everything dear to a pure and a generous nature. But it is a crown of life which the apostle holds out as the reward of enduring temptation. Surely this is a recompense more than sufficient to make amends for all the self-denial and pain of the endurance. The conflict and the sorrow are but for a moment; the crown and the bliss are to be eternal.

The Redeemer himself, through St. John in the Revelation, has uttered these cheering words: "To him that overcometh will I grant to sit with me in my throne." Communion with Christ is the supreme joy of the Christian. Where Christ is, there is heaven. In the passage cited, he promises his people that when the combat is over and the victory won, they shall be with him. "To depart and be with Christ" was Paul's highest ambition. Are you a believer? And can you form a wish beyond this? Yet Christ here promises you more. He promises that you shall not only have your everlasting residence in his presence, but that you shall even share in the glory of his throne. What a mysterious dignity, what an inconceivable exaltation is this!

Whatever else the language of the Saviour may or may not mean, it is doubtless expressive of permanent bliss, as well as supreme honour, in the heavenly state.

To sit with Christ, then, holds out the eternal communion of the blessed with him, their indebtedness to him for their exaltation, and the absolute security of that glorious estate. Now collect these ideas, and give them their united force; remember all of joy, of peace, of elevation, of transport you have ever experienced in the communion of the Redeemer: strip these emotions of all drawbacks arising from our present condition: raise them to their utmost conceivable height: and crown them with a safety that fears no alarms, and a duration that dreads no end:—and what can be wanting to complete your bliss? Sin is gone. Temptation is over. Death is past. Sorrow is forgotten. Danger is removed. Joy is complete. Peace reigns. Eternal life is begun. The song is raised. God, and saints, and angels are your companions for ever. Can you frame a conception of a more glorious state? Can you feel a desire for any higher felicity?

Yet a higher is here promised to his saints by our ascended and loving Redeemer. They shall sit with him *in his throne*, shall have a share in his regal dignity. All that is comprehended in this astonishing promise, no man, perhaps no angel, knows. When our Divine Redeemer undertakes to elevate his redeemed ones, he will do such things as none can anticipate. But one thing we know, —that there is a close and mysterious union between Christ and his regenerated people. When he died, they died in him. When he rose from the dead, they rose in him. When he went up to glory, they ascended in his person. Here the idea of this union is carried still further, in the declaration that they shall sit with him in his throne;—he as the royal bridegroom, they as the crowned and happy bride. There is a glorious significance in the words, which is hidden from our present knowledge, but reserved for the blessed experience of all those who endure to the end.

There is one more thought contained in this promise, which must not be omitted; for it is equally honouring to Christ and precious to his people. It is, that all this dignity, which an apostle, as if labouring for words to express the fulness of his meaning, has called "an exceeding weight of glory," is the gift of grace. "To him that overcometh will I grant it," says the condescending Redeemer. As Mediator, he bestows it. As King of Zion, he confers, with sovereign authority, the honours of his own kingdom. And his gift conveys an authentic, indubitable, and inalienable title to the heavenly inheritance.

Do we require strong encouragement? Do we need mighty succours? Must we be cheered, amid our trials, by divine reliefs, and sustained by infinite props? Surely, here, in the promise of a heavenly crown and a joint occupancy of the Redeemer's throne, we have all that can be desired or conceived.

A Still Further Encouragement to the Believer in Temptation is the Victory of Christ.

"I also overcame," is the clarion note, in which he calls his followers to the combat. Christian soldier! can you think it hard to follow where the Captain of your salvation has gone before you? Christian sufferer! can you murmur, when called to endure trials in such company? Remember that Christ was tempted in all points, even as you are. From the plague of the heart he was, indeed, free; but, in all else, he bore your burdens. He was tempted by the devil to desert the contest, and make void his coming and work as Mediator. But he overcame. Supported by the power of his own Divinity, cheered by the presence of the Father, and filled with the influences of the Holy Spirit, he met his combined foes, and "made a show of them openly." The same power of Christ, the same presence of the Father, and the same energy of the Spirit are yours, as they were his. They are provided for you, and made over to you in the covenant. In the strength which they afford, you are called to combat. Let the victory of your leader give you victory also.

The Final Ground of Encouragement to the Christian under Temptation is the Pledge which he has in the Reward of the Redeemer.

The recompense secured to him by "overcoming," he thus declares himself: "I am set down with my Father in his throne." The recompense which he promises to his followers for "overcoming" is: "They shall sit with me in my throne." Reader, as surely as the exaltation of Christ followed his victory, so surely shall eternal glory crown your triumph. As certainly as the Father was faithful in his promise to the Son, so certainly will the Son be faithful in his promise to you. Christ engaged under covenant promises peculiar to his relation as Mediator; you have enlisted under covenant promises peculiarly suited to your relation as his disciple and follower. The promises to Christ have been fulfilled long ages ago; the promises to you shall be fulfilled in their season. Lift up the eye of faith. Let down the anchor of hope. Let the tendrils of love, shooting across the gulf, fasten, with firm grasp, upon the heavenly inheritance. Fix your exultant view upon the wreath which waits for you in heaven. Think how sweet it will be to put off the harness of battle; to wipe the dust and sweat from your victorious brow; and to receive from the King of saints, your own loved and loving Redeemer, the laurel and the throne.

There is strength in this meditation. There are seeds of victory in it. There are resources wrapped up in it against the power of every temptation and the fierceness of every conflict.

CHAPTER XI.

DELIVERANCE OUT OF TEMPTATION SURE TO THE GODLY.

In their weakness, dependence, and ignorance, but especially in their judgments of the Divine works and ways, men are but children. Of the doings of the Almighty, how small a part are submitted to any human eye. Yet, with the experience of a span and a survey narrowed to microscopic proportions, we presume to judge the Infinite One. God is not thus to be measured. His plans are like himself, vast, far-reaching, and incomprehensible. Our false judgments do not disturb him. Nothing hastens, nothing retards, nothing can defeat his purposes.

Wicked men perpetually misjudge God. Refusing the light of his word, they form their opinions by their own weak and blinded powers. From these false judgments they draw conclusions fatal to themselves. "Because judgment against an evil work is not executed speedily, therefore the hearts of the sons of men are fully set in them to do evil." They deny the fulfilment of God's promises. They set at naught his threatenings. And, in the delirium of a momentary impunity, they cry: "Where is the promise of his coming?"

But it is not the wicked alone, who misinterpret the Deity. With all their advantage of better knowledge, God's own people are prone to the folly of hasty and rash judgments. His providence has often proved a stumbling-block to them. Hear Asaph declaring: "Verily, I have cleansed my heart in vain, and washed my hands in innocency." Hear Jeremiah remonstrating: "Wherefore doth the way of the wicked prosper? Wherefore are they happy that deal very treacherously?" Hear the chosen people, in the time of Malachi exclaiming: "It is a vain thing to serve God."

The perplexity lies in this—that the wicked often prosper, while the righteous are in trouble. But let it be considered, in the first place, that the splendour of the wicked is but a mere outward shining, while to the godly even the scantiest worldly portion is sweetened by the promises of God's grace. Let it be considered, secondly, that, though we grant the worst, the Scripture meets the difficulty by teaching us to enlarge our views of the Divine procedure, and to extend the ground upon which we found our conclusions as to the accomplishment of both promises and threatenings.

Indeed, the perplexity is completely solved, all darkness is lifted from the subject, and the whole economy of God's procedure towards the righteous and the wicked is placed in the clearest light, in a single passage from St. Peter's Second Epistle, (chap. ii. ver. 9,) wherein he declares that "the Lord knoweth how to deliver the godly out of temptations, and to reserve the unjust unto the day of judgment to be punished." Here we have the assurance that, despite all present appearances to the contrary, God's faithfulness will, in the end, be conspicuously displayed, on the one hand, in the deliverance of the godly, and, on the other, in the punishment of the wicked.

The Lord knoweth how to deliver the godly out of temptation. It is taken for granted here that the godly may be, and often are, subjected to trials: which, as we have seen, is the proper meaning of the word "temptations." To such an extent, indeed, is this true, that there have been few eminent saints who have not been at the same time eminent sufferers. Besides the ordinary evils of life, believers have trials peculiar to themselves; trials arising from the malice of Satan, the allurements of the world, and the motions of indwelling sin. Several things are implied in this promised deliverance out of temptation. Thus,

God Knows and Considers the Trials of His People.

A physician must be acquainted with the nature of his patient's disease; its causes, progress, and strength. Our God is thus acquainted with all our temptations. He has marked their beginning, and observed their course. He can trace every tear to its source. He knows each complaint before it is uttered.

God Holds in His Control the Issues of our Trials.

"The Lord reigneth" with an authority sovereign and universal. The machine of providence is vast and complicated; but the Divine Artificer knows every movement, and governs every spring and wheel. Were it otherwise, did God deliver nature and providence to the domination of mere general laws, the assurance of deliverance would be without meaning or comfort to individual sufferers. But the doctrine of a particular providence gives to all such an assurance of inestimable value, an assurance most precious and consolatory.

God Purposely Permits Trials to Overtake his People for their Discipline and Growth in Grace.

Evil, from whatever source derived, springs not up from the ground. It comes from the hand of the Lord. He it is who lays affliction upon our loins. Not only do the evils of physical nature,—losses by the elements, the death of friends, our own sickness, &c.,—proceed from God; but even those evils, in which the agency of our fellow-men is concerned, are represented in the Divine word as overtaking us by his providence. He does not, indeed, originate that deluge of evils which desolates the world; but he marks its progress, directs its course, and controls its issue. A Christian is, therefore, to view every adverse event as sent to him from heaven, and as bringing with it this message: "Hear ye the rod and him that hath appointed it."

God will Conduct all the Trials of the Godly to a Happy Issue.

The godly are objects of the Divine love; and this, of itself, is enough to secure their ultimate happiness. The argument here is short and plain. Love, by a necessity of its nature, seeks the good of its object, and, if able, always secures it. Therefore, unless the power of Christ fails, his people shall pass safely and triumphantly through all temporal evils. Moreover, their sins are forgiven; and they shall, therefore, in the end, be set free from all sin's direful consequences. "Many are the afflictions of the righteous, but the Lord delivereth him out of them all."

The Providence of God, no less than His Word, assures to the Godly Deliverance out of Temptation.

This animating and comforting truth shines conspicuously in God's dealings towards his people. What age or country has witnessed the perils of God's people, and has not witnessed their deliverance? Two signal instances are cited by Peter as confirming the doctrine;—the first, that of Noah delivered from the deluge; the second, that of Lot delivered out of Sodom.

Noah was a tempted, that is, a tried, saint. The enormities of a world ripe for destruction met him on every side. Rapine stalked the earth, and marked its path with blood. Giants in crime, as well as in stature, contended for the precedence in iniquity. Violence, oppression, lust, and anarchy had deformed and wasted the face of society. The traditions of truth were lost. Even the light of nature had sunk amid the gathering darkness. To the heart of a holy man this scene must have been a daily anguish; to the eye of a prophet it presented a portentous spectacle. That judgments were on the wing, he might have conjectured even before those dreadful words were spoken in his ear: "I will destroy all flesh with the earth." Noah heard in them the fiat of doom. Every man he knew, every dwelling he entered, every object he beheld, was devoted to extermination. Every passing cloud held up the monition of approaching ruin. Wrath muttered in the thunder, and moaned in every blast. In this sore "temptation" his faith rested on God, and was answered by a miracle. The ruin, long suspended, came at last. Down from the skies and up from the great deep it came, till towers and cities were submerged—till islands and continents disappeared—till the everlasting hills under the whole heavens became the channels of the sea. Then faith rode sublime; the treasure of the world's virtue floated secure above the mountains; and the same solemn hour witnessed a signal exhibition of both the goodness and severity of God. Thus the godly man was delivered out of his "temptation;" and his history remains, like those relics still seen upon the mountain tops, an imperishable memorial of the Divine truth and faithfulness.

From this wide theatre of the Divine judgments, let us turn to one more narrow, but not less striking, in the burning plains of Palestine. There, amidst the solitude of surrounding sands, lies a deep and stagnant lake. No sea birds haunt the sedge upon its shores. No sail of busy merchant plies its leaden surface. No song of cheerful mariner echoes from its solitary margin. When the wind has, with difficulty, ruffled its sluggish waters, their hollow murmur sounds like the voices of some confused multitude struggling beneath its waves. This land of saltness and of death is the place where Sodom stood. Here the cities of the plain lifted their domes and towers and palaces towards heaven. Here God rained upon sinners a tempest of fire. But even when the Divine anger broke through the course of nature, the sky held up its wrathful store, till angels had come down, and led away from the descending ruin the only righteous man who had his dwelling there. While setting up his blazing beacon to the world, the God of vengeance knew how to deliver the godly out of temptations.

The latter clause of the passage cited contains a solemn warning to the wicked. "The Lord knoweth how to reserve the unjust to the day of judgment to be punished." He knows how to "*reserve*" them. A word of pregnant import, denoting secure and absolute control. If a king were said to reserve certain rebels against a fixed day, we should understand that he was no longer in conflict with them for his throne; but that he had broken their designs, had gained possession of their persons, and had determined, at a fitting opportunity, to bring them forth to receive their sentence.

Thus the Holy Ghost, by the pen of the apostle Peter, warns the ungodly that God knows how to "reserve" them for punishment. They may, indeed, long go unpunished. The young heir may plunge into riot and dissipation. The deceiver may spread his lines, and catch his prey, and revel in the spoils. The son of ambition may devise his plan, push his means, extend his influence, seize the reins of power, and rule without check from God or man. The wicked may combine and prosper. A world of sinners may add crime to crime, till they fill the groaning earth with wrong and outrage. But the day of reckoning will come at length, when He who sits on high will bring the madness of his enemies to an end, and summon them before the bar of judgment.

This solemn truth the apostle illustrates by the instances of the fallen angels, the antediluvian world, and the inhabitants of Sodom.

In regard to the first of these examples: if God spared not the sons of the morning, but blasted all their glory, what hope is left for sinners of an earth-born origin? In regard to the second: when was sin ever allowed a wider range? When did vengeance more profoundly sleep? Yet the flood came, and swept them all away. In regard to the third: Sodom's blazing beacon shines through all the intervening ages, and sheds down its warning light on this distant clime and period.

These histories are written for our learning, on whom the ends of the world are come. The punishment of the sinning angels and the overthrow of the cities of the plain proclaim the certainty of the destruction of transgressors. The ruins of the old world call upon us from the heights of the mountains, call upon us from the depths of the earth, to beware of trusting to a temporary respite, and dreaming of impunity amidst the mines and batteries of the Divine justice. That justice reserves the unjust to the day of judgment to be punished. The day of judgment! How earthly interests fade and wither at the sound. The day of judgment! How human tribunals vanish, as the great white throne appears. The day of judgment! How, at thought of it the boast of the blasphemer dies upon his tongue. The day of judgment! How the mask of the hypocrite falls and the sophistries of the skeptic are dumb, when its light streams in upon the soul. The day of judgment! At the stupendous conception, time shrinks into a span; earth dwindles to a point; and the hoarded treasures of both become lighter than the small dust of the balance. Reader, may that solemn day find, for you and for me, in the Judge upon its burning throne, a Friend, a Brother, an Advocate!

CHAPTER XII.

THE METHODS WHEREBY THE GODLY ARE DELIVERED OUT OF TEMPTATION.

Dr. South, in his able sermon on this subject, has enumerated, as comprehensive of all, three Divine ways of deliverance from temptation, viz. 1. Of being kept from it; 2. Of being supported under it; and 3. Of being brought out of it. I shall attempt, in this chapter, little beyond a reproduction, in a condensed form and under a modern garb, of the excellent remarks of that distinguished prelate.

God Delivers his People out of Temptation by Keeping them at a Distance from it and not Suffering them to be Assailed by it.

This prevention of temptation, this keeping of it off from the soul, is, doubtless, the surest, and, therefore, the best, defence against it. As distance from danger is the most effective shelter from it, so distance from temptation is the strongest rampart against it. A secure barrier is thus reared between the soul and the approaches of its enemy. How many lapses would Israel have been spared, had God prevented the approach of the Midianitish women! How many scars would Job have escaped, if Satan had been by the Divine arm held back from the assault!

For this reason, preventing grace ought to be looked upon as a most signal token of the Divine mercy. Doubtless it is an eminent act of grace to restore a believer who has fallen, but it would have been a more eminent one to keep him from falling; just as it is better not to break a limb, than to have it set and healed after it has been broken. Happy, therefore, beyond the common happiness of Christians, are they who, in all their Christian course, are so guarded and watched over that their deliverance is effected rather by rescue than by recovery. "I will guard thee with mine eye," said God to the holy Psalmist. Next to the protecting shelter of God's wing, is the securing prospect of his eye.

Numerous are the deliverances wrought for us, which we see; but more numerous far are those which we do not see. How often is our destruction plotted by the tempter! How often are his nets spread for us in secret, and we go securely treading towards our ruin, till some preventing providence arrests us in our career, and draws back our foot from the fatal snare!

If we closely observe the actings of the heart, we shall find that temptation wins upon it by small, secret, and almost imperceptible gradations. Its encroachments are so strangely insinuating, that no security under it is for a moment to be compared with being at a distance from it. If, therefore, we hate its intimacy, let us dread its acquaintance, and shun its converse. For he who would gain a complete victory over it, must know that to grapple with it is at best but a venture, while to fly from it is certain victory.

How much sin does God's grace prevent by cutting off the opportunities of sin! How many might have stolen as Achan did, if a wedge of gold had been placed within their reach! How many might have repeated David's adultery and murder, if they had been tried by David's circumstances! How many might have shared the guilt of Peter's fall, if they had met with Peter's surprise! How much of the innocence of the world is nothing more than want of opportunity to do the wickedness, to which men are inclined! What numbers forbear sinning, not because God's grace has wrought upon their wills, but because God's providence has kept them aloof from the occasions of sin!

God Delivers His People out of Temptation by so Succouring and Supporting them, after they have Entered into the State of Temptation, that they Emerge from it Unharmed.

A man may be said to enter into temptation when he meets with such objects, or is brought into such circumstances as are peculiarly fitted to draw forth the workings of his natural corruption; and especially of that particular corruption which is strongest and most predominant in him. Thus a proud and aspiring man has entered into the state of temptation when he has attained to honours suited to his pride and ambition; a covetous man has entered into temptation when he meets with opportunities of gain calculated to feed and gratify his love of money; and so in regard to other passions and appetites, which rule and dominate in the hearts of men. When the objects or incentives adapted to kindle and inflame their several lusts are present to their senses, their standing is slippery; and what the issue will be God only knows, to whose power alone it belongs to bring them, as it were, out of the jaws of death, and so to effect their deliverance.

Now, it is possible that, by peculiar grace, a believer so situated may come out of the temptation without in the least degree yielding to it or being tainted by it. But this is a rare case, and the result not to be attained but by a power infinite and divine. For, as it was God who suspended the force of that material fire which was kindled in the furnace of Dura to consume the three Hebrew youths, so it is God alone who can control the fury of this spiritual flame, and keep it from seizing upon the soul, in whose carnal and corrupt affections there is always so much fuel for it to fasten and prey upon. Yet God has not left us without some signal examples of a grace so pre-eminent and glorious. Joseph, tempted by the alluring though shameful solicitations of Potiphar's wife; Moses, tempted by the prospect of a crown; David, tempted by the opportunity of taking the life of a rival, who alone stood in his way to a throne; Daniel and his three friends, tempted by the terror of death in forms the most dreadful to nature; and Paul and Barnabas, tempted by the proffer of divine honours;—these persons, though all subjected to the power of the mightiest temptations, yet came out of them not in the least tainted or overcome by them. Whence it is evident that God secures his children against temptation, not only by prevenient grace which keeps them from it, but also by supervenient grace which supports them under it, and brings them victorious out of it.

God Delivers His People out of Temptation, by Enabling them to Resist, and finally to Triumph over it, even after they have been in some measure Prevailed upon by it.

God's methods of deliverance in this case are characterized by no little variety. Sometimes he simply permits evil to enter into the thoughts of his people, but delivers them from a frequent and complacent revolving of it in the mind. Sometimes he allows the temptation to proceed to this length also, but hinders it from coming to a full consent and purpose of the will. At other times he suffers it to take possession of the will, but even then stifles it, as it were, in the birth, and keeps it from breaking forth into the actual commission of sin. And, finally, for reasons known to his own sovereignty, but inscrutable to all finite understanding, he sometimes permits a temptation to become so powerful, and to prevail to such a degree, as to break out into open and even flagrant transgression. But, by a mighty and invincible grace, he ever curbs and restrains its insolence, so that it never gains entire, absolute, and final conquest over the elect. It may swell and rage, but its dominion is broken. It may bruise and wound, but it shall never kill. The Spirit of God will interpose to prevent such an issue. The promise remains sure and steadfast to all who are in the state of grace, that "sin shall not have dominion over them." And of this, let the recovery of David and of Peter, after having so grievously and deeply fallen, serve both as an example and a demonstration.

CHAPTER XIII.

THE LESSONS OF TEMPTATION.

THE subject we have been considering has many important issues of a practical character. Let the reader direct his attention to the following; and may the Holy Spirit impress them upon all hearts.

The Doctrine of Temptation Teaches Believers not to be Amazed when they are called to pass through Trials.

Peter, in his First Epistle, exhorts the Christians of his day in these words: "Beloved, think it not strange concerning the fiery trial, which is to try you, as though some strange thing happened unto you." Affliction is the common lot of God's chosen ones. Losses, bereavements, pains, calumnies, reproaches, direct solicitations to sin,—in a word, trials of various name,—are the footsteps of the flock. Many are the Marahs, many the waters of bitterness, of which the children of God, as well as the children of the Evil One, are called to drink. "In the world ye shall have tribulation," is the Master's word to his disciples. Temptation, therefore, will certainly come. It is threatened to the old man; it is promised to the new. It is a part of the believer's heritage, both as a child of sin and a child of grace. Let him not, then, look upon his afflictions as something strange, nor be surprised at them as at some unexpected event. Though they may be sharp and fiery, they are still for trial only, and not for destruction. They are designed but to test his sincerity, his strength, his patience, his confidence in God.

The Doctrine of Temptation Teaches a Lesson of Patience.

Murmuring at the waters of Marah only increases our own sorrow. No consolation ever came by fretting. This offends God; shuts out the sunlight; blights the spirit; withers the strength. Reader, learn not to be impatient under the burden. Bear it you must and shall. If you fret and wrestle, it will but gall you the more. On the other hand, the more quietly you submit, the less you will have to suffer. Murmurer, go and contemplate Jesus,—meek, calm, resigned, patient, though bending under a load of sorrow, such as you have never been called to bear. Why should you complain, when you can pass no turn or station in all the way which was not a weeping-place to your Saviour before you?

This Doctrine Teaches a Lesson of Dependence.

Our strength is not in ourselves. It comes from a higher source. God is the strength of our heart. With him are power and might. To him all cases, all difficulties, are alike. Nothing is great with

God; nothing intricate; nothing hard. He can as well help us, and is as willing to help us, in a great trial as in a small. "It is nothing with thee," said the pious Asa, addressing himself to the Strength of Israel, "it is nothing with thee to help, whether with many, or with them that have no power." In every trial, the grace of God is alone sufficient to enable us to endure. This must be sought. This must be relied on. This must be honoured. Without Christ we can do nothing.

The Doctrine of Temptation Teaches a Lesson of Humility.

Where is boasting? Surely every man is vanity. His strength is the strength of an infant. Well may his loftiness be bowed down; his haughtiness made low; and his pride laid in the dust. He has in himself nothing whereof he may glory. "Self must be humbled, pride abased." The lower self sinks, the higher faith rises; for faith is just the dependence of weakness on strength, of ignorance on wisdom, of guilt on righteousness, of unworthiness on merit.

There is a Lesson of Faith and Hope in this Doctrine.

An old writer has well said: "God had one Son without sin; but he never had one without sorrow." Stumble not, therefore, at the dispensation of trial. The circumstances of trial differ with different believers; but one thing in common they all have. They are all tried. They are all subjected to discipline. They are all brought into the school of experience. "God sits as a refiner and purifier of silver." He is to be viewed as such in all the trials he brings upon us. "The refiner does not put his gold into the furnace, because he values it less than the dross, which lies on one side; but because he values it he puts it in, in order to purify it." This way of sorrow,—that is, of trial, of temptation,—is the way in which all the children of God must walk. It is the King's highway, the royal road, which leads to the land where sorrow is unknown. "No cross, no crown." Therefore, beloved Christians, learn to have faith in God. Trust him for a happy issue to every trial. "The Lord knoweth how to deliver the godly out of temptations." He has his own time, and he will take his own way; but, if you are his children, he will surely deliver you. The covenant of grace, the word of promise, and the experience of the church, all encourage you to trust in the Lord. Who has ever seen God's people brought into the fire and the flood, and has not seen them brought forth at length into a wealthy place? They looked unto him and were lightened; and their faces were not ashamed.

There is a Lesson of Courage in the Doctrine of Temptation.

Fear not, beloved, because you have such a road to travel. Turn not aside because the way is rough. Be strong in the grace that is in Christ Jesus. If there is a roaring lion that seeks to devour, there is a rescuing lion that will certainly deliver;—the Lion of the tribe of Judah. "The God of peace will bruise Satan under your feet shortly." Remarkable here are both the words and the sense. It is not said that believers shall bruise Satan under their feet, but that God will. Again, it is not said that God will bruise Satan under his own feet, but under theirs. There is a deep significance, a pregnant meaning, here. The victory will be theirs, though wrought by God. The strength in which they conquer is Divine. And this will be "shortly." Wait a while, and it shall be done. Fear not, then, while you have such a helper. And remember that the blessedness spoken of in the passage so often cited from St. James, in the foregoing pages, is affirmed, not of the man who escapes temptation, but of him who "endures" it; of him who stands up erect under it; of him who comes unscathed out of it; of him who endures "as seeing him who is invisible," looking not at the things that are seen, which are temporal, but at the things that are not seen, which are eternal.

Temptation has even a Lesson of Joy for those who fall into it.

Paradoxical as this may seem, it is yet distinctly taught in the Scripture. We have the testimony of three apostles to this point.

Paul affirms: "Tribulation worketh experience; and experience, hope; and hope maketh not ashamed; because the love of God is shed abroad in our hearts by the Holy Ghost, which is given unto us." Experience of God's grace, hope in his mercy, trust in his faithfulness, and his love shed abroad in the heart through the gift and working of the Holy Spirit,—do not these things form a solid foundation for Christian joy? Yet they are all the fruit of sanctified trials.

James exhorts: "My brethren, count it all joy, when ye fall into divers temptations." "Philosophy (says good Matthew Henry) may instruct men to be calm under their troubles; but Christianity teaches them to be joyful: because such exercises proceed from love, and not fury, in God. In them we are conformable to Christ our head, and they become marks of our adoption. By suffering in the ways of righteousness, we are serving the interests of our Lord's kingdom among men, and edifying the body of Christ; and our trials will brighten our graces now, and our crown at last. Therefore there is reason to count it all joy, when trials and difficulties become our lot in the way of our duty. And this is not purely a New Testament paradox, but, even in Job's time, it was said, Behold, happy is the man whom God correcteth."

Peter exhorts the believers of his day to rejoice even amid fiery trials, inasmuch as they were thereby made partakers of the sufferings of Christ, and had the assurance that, when his glory should be revealed, they should be glad also with exceeding joy. Surely Christians have abundant occasion for rejoicing in their trials, in that therein and thereby they have fellowship with Christ both in his sufferings and his glory. The sufferings of Christ's members are, in a most important sense, his own. He suffers in them. He feels their pains, bears their infirmities, and sympathizes in their sorrows. Herein they are made conformable to him. "Christians ought not only to be patient, but to rejoice, in their sharpest and sorest sufferings for Christ, because they are tokens of the Divine favour; they promote the gospel, and prepare for glory. They who rejoice in their sufferings for Christ, shall eternally triumph and rejoice with him in glory." (*Henry.*)

The Doctrine of Temptation conveys an Impressive Lesson of Charity.

When we consider both our own weakness, and the number, power, and craft of our enemies, the wonder is, not that so many fall, but that so many stand. Indeed, no man stands, except as he is held up by Divine power. "By the grace of God," may every one say who has been enabled to endure temptation, "by the grace of God I am what I am." Reader, if thou hast weathered the storm, while another has bent to the blast, who maketh thee to differ? And what hast thou of strength or virtue that thou didst not receive? Thy endurance of temptation, thy resistance of the world, the flesh, and the devil, is all of grace.

The victory is Christ's, though the triumph and the benefit are thine.

None know either the weakness of nature, or the force of temptation, as well as He who, though without sin, was in all points tempted even as we are; and surely none was ever so lenient and tender in his judgments of others. "Woman, hath no man condemned thee? Neither do I condemn thee; go and sin no more." Incomparable words! Blessed Jesus! charity was not a name upon thy lips, but a reality in thy heart. However much the fallen may have sinned in yielding to the fierce assaults of temptation, I cannot doubt that the unfallen often sin more in the sight of God by their harsh judgments and their uncharitable speeches.

"Let no man in his Prayers Peremptorily Importune God for any Particular Enjoyment or State of Life; that is, let him not Pray and Prescribe to God in the same Petition.*

"God alone knows what will help and what will hurt us. He only can discern the various windings and turnings, the peculiar bent and constitution of the heart, and how this or that thing would affect or work upon it, and how far such or such a condition would agree or disagree with it. He knows the proper suitableness and unsuitableness of every state of life to each mind and temper, which it is hardly possible for the ablest and deepest

* This head and the following are taken from Dr. South's third Sermon on Temptation. The points, as will be seen, are admirably handled by that eminent author.

heads to have a perfect knowledge of. For such very often pray for they know not what, even for their own bane and ruin, and with equal importunity and ignorance solicit their own destruction. They think they ask for bread, but it proves a stone; and for a fish, but they find and feel it to be a serpent; and, therefore, it is oftentimes in mere love to their persons that God answers not their prayers. In a word, the wisest man living is not wise enough to choose for himself, and therefore we have cause to fly to an infinite wisdom to direct our request, as well as to an infinite goodness to supply our wants.

"As a man is by no means Positively to Request or Pray for any Particular Enjoyment or State of Life, so ought he, with the greatest Satisfaction of Mind, to Accept of and Acquiesce in that State and Condition (whatsoever it be), which Providence shall think fit to allot and set out for him.

"I have already shown that no man living is in this case fit to choose for himself. And if we refer it to God to choose for us, surely there is all the reason in the world that we should stand to this choice. We come all as suppliants, or rather as beggars, to the throne of grace; and to beg and to choose too, we know is too much. Is thy condition in the world poor, thy circumstances low, and thy fortune, in the eyes of all about thee, mean and contemptible? Repine not at it; for do we not, every day, beg of God not to lead us into temptation? And shall we not allow him to judge which is the best and surest way to keep us from it?

Possibly this very thing that thou complainest of is that by which God is effectually answering that prayer. He denies thee honour, but it is perhaps because he intends thee heaven. He refuses thee greatness, but it may be to preserve thy innocence, and, perchance, in the long run, thy neck too. In a word, he withholds that from thee which he knows thy spiritual strengths are not able to bear. Thou affectest to be high and powerful, and probably the tempter, who hates thee mortally, would be glad to have thee so too. But God, who thoroughly knows and truly loves thee, knows that, instead of being high or powerful, it is much better for thee to be harmless and safe. And if there be any truth in the gospel, and all religion be not made up of tricks and lies, it is really better and more eligible for a man to keep a good conscience, though with a halter about his neck, or a dagger at his throat, than with the loss of it to gain all the riches and glories and kingdoms of this world, which the tempter, heretofore, so liberally offered our Saviour, and our Saviour so resolutely and disdainfully threw back in his face. In fine, we have nothing to do but to commit ourselves to God, 'as to a faithful Creator,' to receive what he assigns us humbly, and to enjoy it thankfully, knowing that, by denying us these gaudy nothings, these gilded poisons, he is doing us the greatest kindness in the world, which (in answer to the Lord's prayer), is to 'keep us from temptation,' and by keeping us from temptation, to 'deliver us from evil,' and by delivering us from evil, to prepare and fit us for all the good that can be prayed for, and for himself, the endless, inexhaustible fountain of it; 'in whose presence there is fulness of joy, and at whose right hand there are pleasures for evermore.' "

A word of Encouragement and Exhortation to Christians under Trial shall Close this Detail of the Lessons to be Drawn from the Doctrine of Temptation, as set forth in Holy Scripture.

My afflicted brother! stumble not at the dispensation of trial. Think it not strange concerning the fiery trial, which has already, to some extent, tried you, and which may, in the providence of God, be commissioned to try you yet further, as though some strange thing happened unto you. Say not, "Why am I thus? Why do I meet with such things? Why has the Almighty permitted them to befall me?" These are the footsteps of the flock. Of the blessed in heaven it is said: "These are they which came out of great tribulation." They were all tempted. They were all tried. Remember the words of the Lord Jesus: "What I do, thou knowest not now, but thou shalt know hereafter." If God hear your prayer, and grant you a speedy deliverance, praise him for his goodness. But if otherwise, seek a submission that knows neither distress nor repining. It is well with the righteous. It is well with him always. It is well with him under all circumstances.

Take refuge in God. Your chief recourse in the

hour of trial must be to him. All other consolations are but insignificant rills. God is the fountain. The balm which alone can heal your sore is found in Gilead. The Physician who only can apply it with unerring skill is there also. Look through all second causes up to the great First Cause. Recognize God's hand in the stroke that has fallen upon you. See Divine wisdom and love united in mingling the ingredients of the bitter cup. All your hope and all your help are in God. Fear not while you are in his hands. He brought his people to the Red Sea. He subjected them to sore trial there. Mountains hemmed them in on either side; the enemy urged them from behind; and a gloomy waste of waters lowered upon them in front. But Jehovah spake, and opened a path through the flood. Trust God fully, then. Trust him in the storm. Trust him through the storm. Trust him where you cannot trace him. That is best for you which is best for your soul. That is most helpful to you which most helps you on towards heaven. Let God be the Judge. Do not even wish the wheels of providence turned from their course. Rest assured that those wheels are moved by infinite power, and guided by infinite wisdom. After the tempest comes the sunshine. Whatever is gone, the promise of a faithful God is left.

Remember that life is a warfare, a long struggle, against innumerable foes. Listen reverently, listen in an obedient and loyal temper, to that voice which shall judge you at the last day: "To him that overcometh will I grant to sit with me in my throne, even as I overcame, and am set down with my Father in his throne." Let that word sink into your heart; for, if you know not what it is to resist, how shall you attain the meed of them that conquer?

CHAPTER XIV.

THE TEMPTATION OF PETER.

In the temptation of the apostle Peter, we have one of the most humiliating, and, at the same time, one of the most instructive events recorded in the New Testament. It is an event worthy to be treasured in the memory. The seasonable recollection of it may serve to abate pride, to check presumption, to cheer despondency, to teach us our own weakness, and to remind us of the Master's grace.

The History of this Memorable Temptation, briefly traced, is as follows:

The first day of the Jewish passover had closed. In the evening of that day, all the families of Jerusalem were accustomed at the same hour to partake of the paschal supper, a festival at once solemn and cheerful. As night shut in, our Lord and his apostles assembled in an upper chamber, prepared for their reception. It was the evening which preceded his crucifixion, and this was his last interview with his disciples before that awful tragedy. His tenderness for them, shaded with anticipations of his own approaching passion, gave a surpassing interest to the occasion. He drew aside the veil of the immediate future, and showed them what must shortly happen. As the sad scenes rose in succession before his view, especially the treachery of Judas, a sorrowful emotion crossed his bosom; and, looking upon the twelve, "he was troubled in spirit, and testified and said, Verily, verily, I say unto you, that one of you shall betray me."

This introduced the subject of his separation from the disciples: "Little children, yet a little while I am with you. Ye shall seek me; and, as I said unto the Jews, whither I go ye cannot come, so now I say to you." The suspense in which these words left him, ill suited the ardent and impetuous spirit of Peter, and he inquired, "Lord, whither goest thou?" Jesus replied, "Whither I go thou canst not follow me now, but thou shalt follow me afterwards." Peter asks again, "Why cannot I follow thee now? I will lay down my life for thy sake."

These words, which betray an overweening self-confidence, are the key to all that follows. Peter repeated them at the Mount of Olives: "Though all men should be offended because of thee, yet will I never be offended." Thereupon our Lord reiterated his former asseveration: "I tell thee, Peter, the cock shall not crow till thou hast denied me thrice."

The agony of the garden was immediately followed by the treachery of Judas and the apprehension of the Saviour. On that occasion, the apostle seemed ready to make good his boast. He drew his sword, and, opposing himself singly against a band of armed soldiers, prepared to contend for his Master's liberty and life. But what was his amazement when Jesus forbade all resistance, and he beheld him whom the wind and the sea had obeyed, bound like a felon, and led away in the midst of his enemies! Upon this he fled; but, soon escaping the danger of pursuit, he turned and mingled unnoticed in the crowd that followed Jesus toward the palace of the high priest. He was accompanied by John, who, being known, was admitted without hesitation, and obtained admission for Peter also.

Jesus was now undergoing a preliminary and informal examination at the residence of Caiaphas. It was near midnight, and a fire was kindled in the outer hall, at which a crowd of officers and servants were warming themselves. Peter stood with them for some time unobserved. At length, a maid, belonging to the palace, charged him with being one of Christ's followers. In his surprise and alarm, while all eyes were turned toward him, and before he had a moment's time for reflection, he denied the accusation, adding that he had no knowledge of the prisoner, and did not understand what his accuser meant. He now went out into the vestibule of the palace, and the cock crew. After he returned into the hall, the charge was renewed. A second time he denied, and strengthened his denial with an oath; whereupon the accusation was dropped, and he probably thought the danger over. But, as flight might confirm their suspicions, and as he felt, besides, an earnest wish to see what would be the end of his Master's trial, he continued to sit with the servants, and warmed himself at the fire.

A considerable period must have passed in this manner; during which, the conversation, doubtless, turned on the pretended Messiah and his followers; when another of the company, who had, probably, been eyeing Peter, and perceived that he spoke with the provincial accent peculiar to Galilee, (the least polished district of Palestine,) came forward, and "confidently affirmed, saying, Of a truth, this fellow also was with him."

This accusation, now urged for the third time, and accompanied with presumptive evidence to support it, roused the attention of the whole company. They gathered around Peter, and, with every appearance of crediting the report, said to him, "Surely thou art a Galilean, and thy speech agreeth thereto." At this critical moment, one of the servants, a relation of Malchus, whose ear Peter had stricken off with his sword, added weight to the evidence by saying to him, "Did not I see thee in the garden with him?"

The temptation had now risen to its height. The danger of seizure was imminent, and death seemed involved in the issue. "Then began Peter to curse and to swear, saying, I know not the man; and immediately the cock crew." The Lord Jesus himself was now in the hall, having been brought out from the inner apartment of the palace, after his condemnation. Hearing the awful imprecations of his poor fallen disciple, he "turned and looked upon Peter." There was the man whom he had taken from the nets on the sea of Tiberias, whom he had permitted to be near his person, whom he had dignified with the apostleship, to whom he had showed his glory on the Mount of Transfiguration, who had, a few hours before, eaten of the paschal lamb as a part of his family, whose feet he had washed with his own hands, and who had shared in the parting memorial of his love,—there was this man now standing before him and calling on God to witness that he did not know him. In silent majesty the Lord listened to his curses; and when the wretched man had ended them, he fixed his eye upon this fallen disciple, whose professions of love and devotion had been so loud and repeated. The gaze was earnest, solemn, steady, intolerable. It pierced to the very depths of his being. Peter felt that it was divine. Yet so free was that look from anything even approaching to resentment, so tempered was the beam of the heart-searching God with the goodness of Jesus the Saviour, that, while it shot like lightning into his soul, his soul melted at its touch, and "he went out and wept bitterly."

This History is Full of Instruction.

It Teaches the Deceitfulness of the Human Heart.

No man could be more sincere than Peter was, when he professed a readiness to follow the Master to prison and to death. The image of Jesus in danger produced a yearning of affection, which was instantly followed by the thought of personal sacrifices. He held his life cheap while that image was before him.

But Peter did not know himself. He was all unconscious how much he loved his life; how accessible he was to fear; and how callous that mean passion would render him to all that is tender, sacred, and noble. To what an extent this apostle was self-deceived, we can all now clearly see. But have we learned to distrust ourselves? Despite the complacency which we are apt to feel in our own virtue while it remains untried, have we not reason to fear that much of that treasure which pride loves to count in secret, and vanity to exhibit for admiration, is light gold, and will not bear the scales? Is there not cause to suspect that our inward thoughts of ourselves are higher than they ought to be; and that the very points in which we feel most confident may be precisely those in which we are most likely to fail? Who would have thought that courage and firmness were the qualities in which Peter would prove deficient? a man constitutionally bold, and whom Christ himself had surnamed the "rock?" Yet such is the fact. Let no man, then, think that he knows himself till circumstances have tried him. And let every one of us be assured that there are within us germs of depravity and capabilities of evil which the most diligent scrutiny has failed to discover.

We Learn from this History the Folly and Danger of Self-confidence.

In Peter's boast there was no reference to Divine aid. He seems to have thought that his love and fidelity to the Master were in themselves sufficient to bear him over the fear of death. But "he that trusteth in his own heart is a fool." Our strength is simply God's strength put forth in us. But to realize God's strength, we must trust in God. The most eminent man in the Christian church, furnished with all the gifts and graces befitting the apostolic office, endowed with genius, enriched by learning, schooled by experience, strong in faith, and mighty in the Scriptures, has left on record these memorable words: "not that we are sufficient of ourselves to think anything as of ourselves; but our sufficiency is of God." A great truth, which few will deny in theory; and fewer still, perhaps, ever learn practically, till taught by many painful lessons. Nevertheless, it is vital to Christian growth and steadfastness. The grace of God alone is sufficient. This must be sought; must be relied on; must be honoured by a daily recourse to it, and a daily use of it. Without Christ we can do nothing. With Christ strengthening us, we can do all things.

We see in the Fall of this Apostle the Amazing Power of Temptation.

Peter was constitutionally courageous. He was strongly attached to Christ. He was bound to him by infinite obligations. He was firmly established in the faith that he was the Son of God. He was, moreover, a favoured disciple. He was admitted, with James and John, to be present on several special occasions, when the rest of the twelve were excluded; particularly, on the Mount where Jesus was transfigured. Yet, with all these advantages, he not only fell, but he fell most grievously. Who would have believed that this man, when charged with what ought to have been his glory, would not only shrink from owning his Master, but would disclaim all knowledge of him? He does not even prevaricate, but flatly denies him. He renounces all connection with him and his cause. He calls upon God to bear witness to his falsehood. He invokes curses on himself, to secure the greater credit to his lie.

The power of the temptation is seen in its effects. That which could bring an apostle thus low, may well be dreaded by ordinary Christians. "Let him that thinketh he standeth take heed lest he fall."

We see from the Fall of Peter not only the Power of Temptation, but the Direct Agency of Satan in it.

The power of the temptation in this case was not simply the result of the outward circumstances of the case, urgent as they were; for we have seen men with less grace than Peter had, nay, with no saving grace at all, resist influences more pressing than these. The history of many of the heathen nations furnishes examples of fidelity which vanquished the fear of death. But the outward circumstances were, here, only a vehicle for the unseen power of hell. While the charge assailed Peter without, the devil assaulted him within; and here lay the strength of the trial. "Simon, Simon, Satan has desired to have thee, that he may sift thee as wheat."

These words of our Saviour let us into secrets, which, without Divine revelation, could never have been known. They open to us a glimpse into the spiritual world. Here we see other agency than that of man concerned in human affairs; the events of the world contemplated by other beings than ourselves; and not contemplated merely, but made the subject of actual intercourse between the powers of heaven and hell. Here is the great angel of evil watching an individual man, and, after carefully studying his character, deliberately laying a plan for his destruction, and, as there is reason to think, asking permission of the Ruler of the world to put it into execution. The result shows that the petition was granted, although with a reservation, as in the case of Job, which controlled the issue, and frustrated the ultimate hope of the devil. "I have prayed for thee," said the Saviour, when he warned Peter of the approaching trial, "that thy faith fail not."

A Fifth Lesson, embodied in the Narrative, is the Importance and Value of Christ's Intercession.

When we contemplate the intrinsic enormity of Peter's crime, with its many and great aggravations, and then consider that, instead of receiving from God the just desert of his iniquity, he obtained, in the gift of true repentance, the richest benefit that could be conferred upon him, we may reasonably infer that whatever could avail to procure such a blessing must possess unspeakable value. Our Lord attributes this to his own intercession: "I have prayed for thee." As the great High Priest of the church, Christ presents to the Father the merits of his vicarious obedience and sacrifice, in the form of intercessory prayer, and, since this constitutes the public reason before the universe for the pardon and acceptance of sinners, the blessed Jesus receives the glory of all the benefits conferred on every individual believer from the beginning to the end of the world. While these benefits are gifts of the Father's love, they are granted only through the intercession of him whom the Lord "delighteth to honour." Happy the man who has such an advocate.

We Learn from this History the Necessity and Value of that Preservation which Believers Daily Enjoy.

This, like other common blessings, is too often overlooked, because it is common. My Christian brother, are you a stranger to Peter's anguish? It is only because God has saved you from its cause. If your heart is not the seat of remorse, if you do not blush to look back and tremble to look forward, know that God alone is to be praised. Christ's intercession has prevailed for you, and the Holy Spirit has upheld you by the same unseen but powerful operation by which he upholds the course of nature. We think it too much a matter of course that our faith, hope, and love should continue with us. It is not a matter of course. It is a daily miracle. The Scripture everywhere speaks of it as a glorious result of Divine power. Those who are kept at all, are "kept by the power of God." The apostle speaks of the "exceeding greatness of his power toward them that believe," comparing it to the power by which he raised Christ from the dead. Nothing but the exertion of power like this can preserve a Christian; and in the same degree in which that gracious power is at any time withheld, does the strongest Christian fall, even as Peter did, and pierce himself through with many sorrows.

Peter's Recovery loudly Preaches the Doctrine of the Saints' Perseverance.

The advocates of this doctrine do not pretend

that a saint may not fall. They do not pretend to specify any form or degree of sin he may not commit. All they claim is, that he does not cease to be a Christian, and that he shall never fall into the perdition of hell. And surely the case of Peter is an argument in point. Do the opponents of the doctrine in question maintain that the fall of a Christian into gross immorality proves that he has fallen from grace, and ceased to be a Christian? What immorality can they produce surpassing this sin of Peter? It was directed, as clearly as any sin could be, immediately at his own personal interest in Christ. "I am not one of this man's disciples: I know not the man." This horrid lie, by which he renounced, as far as any act of his could have that effect, all interest in the Saviour, he attested with profane oaths, and that in Christ's very presence. And yet we know, from the lips which cannot lie, that his faith did not fail. Let a stronger case than this be produced, if any such exists. One limitation only do we insist on, viz., that the case be brought out of the record of Holy Scripture; for thus only can we be sure that the persons apostatizing were ever true believers. But, assuredly, among the lapses recorded in Scripture, there is none to equal this. The stability of the covenant, therefore, and of all the hopes which rest upon it, not only remains untouched, but receives fresh confirmation from the memorable scene before us.

This History furnishes a Salutary Caution against a Hasty and Uncharitable Judging of our Brethren.

What conclusion could be more natural in one who had witnessed this conduct of Peter, than that he was a false disciple? What inference more spontaneous than that he was either a hypocrite, who had followed Christ hitherto from the hope of temporal advantage, and who, when this hope was gone, threw off the mask; or that he was, at best, a self-deceiver, who had supposed himself a Christian till he was tried, and was then, for the first time, let into the secret of his true character?

Yet how far, how very far, would either of these judgments have been from the truth! Peter was still a Christian; was beloved of God; was pitied by the Master; was helped by the Spirit; and was, at that very moment, the heir of a heavenly throne. Though he seemed to have utterly forsaken Christ, as one who had neither part nor lot with him, he lived to serve the Master with the purest zeal, and closed a long career of toil, self-denial, and suffering for him, by dying joyfully in his cause. So unable are we to search the heart, or to pierce into the hidden purposes of God. Let us, then, learn to "judge nothing before the time." "Charity hopeth all things."

The Narrative of Peter's Fall and Recovery affords ground of Encouragement to Tempted Believers.

Tempted Christians may here see a truth which, though very plain, is very hard to believe, practically, viz., that their being tried, though it be seventy times seven, argues nothing against their being true believers. When harassed by continual and wearying assaults of the enemy, a man finds it hard to realize his interest in Christ. These temptations stir up his corruption, and make it active; and this brings a cloud over all his evidences of grace. Let a man thus tried remember that he has an apostle in company; that God, while he tenderly loved that apostle, nevertheless suffered Satan to "sift him as wheat;" that the temptation served but to humble him and make him wiser; and that the trial ended in his greater strength and constancy. This is indeed encouraging. Could a Christian feel assured that such would be the fruit of his trials, they would not depress him as they too often do; and he would probably have less of them to endure, because their intended effect would be the sooner realized. We gain nothing by unbelief, but valiant faith "turns to flight the armies of the aliens," and shortens our road to every attainment.

Finally, the History of Peter's Fall opens Sources of Hope to Christians who have Yielded to Temptation and Fallen under its Power.

Let those unhappy Christians who have sunk in the trial find here, in the midst of their misery, an avenue of hope which no man can close. Such persons are apt to give up all for lost; and this is just what the great enemy desires. Whenever they struggle to rise, and would look toward God, the remembrance of their sin returns upon them like a mountain; the adversary urges without remorse the prostrating blow; and they sink down again, weak and weary, in unresisting despondency.

Let such vanquished souls remember Peter. How deeply had he fallen! Yet Christ did not cast away his poor, weak, sinning servant. Christ did not lay up his offence for future judgment, nor spare him only that he might accumulate perdition. No, he pitied him; and, though fallen, he loved him still. He did not forget Peter's love, but kept in store for his servant a bright reversion of better days. He purposed Peter's restoration; and, with a look, he effected it. Oh, fallen Christian! such a look from Jesus will restore you also. While it pierces, it will heal. To this seeming apostate did Christ commit the tenderest and most confidential charge: "Feed my sheep: feed my lambs." And this very man, so vain and self-confident in the chamber, so timid and craven in the garden, so dastardly and impious in the hall, did victorious grace bear through reproaches, and want, and pain, and fiery persecution, to the triumph of a rejoicing crucifixion. From that cross to which he followed his Master, hear him shouting for the victory; and let his voice cheer your desolate and drooping heart. Return once more to Jesus, the Pardoner. Look yet again to Jesus, the Healer. Trust still in Jesus, the Deliverer. Send your cry into the ear and the heart of Jesus, the Restorer. That return, that look, that trust, that cry, shall bring strength into your fainting soul; shall cause your light to break forth as the morning, and your health to spring forth speedily; and shall make righteousness—the imputed righteousness of Christ and the implanted righteousness of the Spirit—to go before you as a defence, and the glory of the Lord to be your rereward.

ALPHABETICAL INDEX OF SUBJECTS.

(The figures refer to the pages.)

www.ingramcontent.com/pod-product-compliance
Lightning Source LLC
LaVergne TN
LVHW021410110826
845150LV00007B/1866

* 9 7 8 1 4 2 5 5 1 1 0 0 5 *